Winners and Losers

PETER LANG
PROMPT

PETER LANG
Oxford • Bern • Berlin • Bruxelles • New York • Wien

Matt Qvortrup

Winners and Losers

Which Countries Are Successful and Why?

PETER LANG
Oxford • Bern • Berlin • Bruxelles • New York • Wien

Bibliographic information published by **Die Deutsche Nationalbibliothek.**
Die Deutsche Nationalbibliothek lists this publication in the "Deutsche Nationalbibliografie"; detailed bibliographic data are available on the Internet at http://dnb.d-nb.de/.

A catalogue record for this book is available from the British Library.

Library of Congress Control Number: 2021018619

A CIP catalog record for this book has been applied for at the Library of Congress.

ISBN 978-1-80079-405-4 (print) • ISBN 978-1-80079-406-1 (ePDF)
ISBN 978-1-80079-407-8 (ePub) • ISBN 978-1-80079-408-5 (mobi)

Published by Peter Lang Ltd, International Academic Publishers, 52 St Giles, Oxford, OX1 3LU, United Kingdom
oxford@peterlang.com, www.peterlang.com

This publication has been peer reviewed.

Shalom

Contents

Tables

Figures

Preface

This short book was written during the Covid-19 lockdown of 2020. The aim was to bring together objective and neutral data and evidence on when countries are successful or not. The short book combines sociology, economics and political science and makes use of statistics to develop the Better Place Index: a measure of success. The book is a snapshot of how things were at a particular period in time. Nothing is static. It is possible that other countries would be winners in the future. Readers who are interested in the methodology and more detailed statistics of each country can look at website, which provides all the information. It can be found at: <https://www.thebetterplaceindex.report/infographics>

The work on the book was made possible through a generous grant from *Guerrand-Hermès Foundation for Peace*, and I would like to thank Dr Scherto R. Gill for facilitating this. The author is also grateful to Mr Mason Waters, my research assistant whose expertise in statistics was invaluable. Chief Simon Pentanu deserves praise for inspiring this study. Further, I want to thank my colleagues Michael Hardy OBE, Richard Dickson, and the Chancellor of my University Margaret Casely-Hayford CBE for support and spirited conversations. I am also grateful to Jens Kromann Kristensen of the World Bank for help and advice. Lastly, I am indebted to Mr Anthony Mason from Peter Lang for facilitating the publication of this short book. The usual caveat applies.

London, 10 February 2021.

Introduction

Statisticians, now over to you, count, measure and compare!

Jean-Jacques Rousseau [1]

The aim of this book is to answer two simple questions: which countries do well and why?

Of course, it is much easier to ask than to answer. First of all, what do we mean by 'well', and how do we answer the 'why'? To deal with the last first, we need a working definition of 'doing well' and we need a benchmark or a yardstick to measure it. We will develop one in this book. We call it the 'Better Place Index' – or BPI for short. It provides a single figure for when countries have low levels of crime and pollution and high levels of health, education and economic prosperity.

However, such a measure only makes constructive sense if it is used to make the world a better place. For this to happen, we need to know when and why some countries do well, and when and why others perform miserably. This is the stuff of many dinner conversations, bar-room chats and learned discourses. Geezers and geniuses have theories about what makes a world a better place. Some blame foreigners for their misery; others give immigrants the credit for having created better societies. Some think it is the welfare state that made their lives better – others think that the 'nanny state' is the root of all evil. The aim here is to be completely open to the 'facts', and unprejudiced as to why a country is likely to come out on top. Previously, we could but use selected examples. Now, in the age of *Big Data*, we can make more scientific judgements based on statistical evidence.

At the time of writing, we have not made the index, we don't know if the winner will be Canada or Cuba, Denmark or the Democratic Republic of Congo, or some other place. Nor do we know if it is a country with high

1 In the French original, '*Calculateurs, c'est maintenant votre affaire*; *comptez*, mesurez, *comparez*, Jean-Jacques Rousseau (1964) Rousseau, J. J. (1964). 'Du contrat social' *Oeuvres completes*. Paris: Pleiade/Gallimard, p. 420.

or low taxation, with many or few emigrants, or if it is a democracy or a state run by a single man (there are very few women dictators!).

So, once we have outlined the index, we look at different factors: accidents of history, and geography, social, economic, political and legal reasons. And we use statistics and facts to prove which factors are conducive for creating a better place.

At the end of the book, we will be able to say not only which countries are 'the better places' (the ones that have success) but also why and when they are likely to achieve this. The conclusions will not be to everyone's liking; we don't like when our pet theories are proven wrong. But to make the world a better place we need to have an open mind. So here we go ....

CHAPTER 1

Which Countries Are Successful?

In 2016, the author of this book was in Bougainville, formally a part of Papua New Guinea. The country was preparing for a vote on independence, and yours truly was there to outline the various options. The Speaker of the Parliament, Chief Simon Pentanu, a soft-spoken giant with a regal demeanour, listened politely, but asked searching and difficult questions. One of them was roughly as follows, 'How exactly do we create a better place?'

My response, using the rather bland jargon of the international consultant, was 'through governance' structures'.

The Chief, still polite, but with a slight overbearing look, responded,

> Sure enough, but sometimes, I'd wish you guys would be more specific. I have to come up with practical ideas and ways to make this a better place. So, I need facts and solid evidence. But, first of all, we need to know what we do well, and then to understand why. That is what I want to know.

At the time, I was not able to provide this 'evidence' and these 'facts'. I promised to go back and look at it. The following pages is, in a sense, an answer to Chief Simon[1], but one that is also of use to everyone else trying to create a successful society. We do this by developing a brand-new ranking; the Better Place Index – or BPI for short.

First the 'doing well' bit. How do we measure success? Today, and for the past seventy years or so, societies have been measured almost solely on economic growth. Generally, politicians, statisticians and others engaged in this have relied on one simple measure for success, namely *Gross Domestic Product* (the value of all goods and services in a country) at *Purchasing*

1 In Papua New Guinea, Chief in an honorary title like 'Sir' in the United Kingdom, and not a sign that the holder is the leader of a tribe.

power parity. The latter is a measure of the relative prices in the different countries. For example, the prize of *A Bloody Mary* in New York is higher than the price of the same drink in Mexico City, but below what it costs in Geneva. Once we take this into account, we get a sense of how well things are going economically.

However, most of us know that there is more to life than economics. Money, I am not going to lie, is, of course, very important. But there are other things that are perhaps equally vital for a good life. This is not just a view shared by hermits and hippies. Even Joseph Stiglitz, the former Chief Economist in the World Bank who – being a bit of an over achiever – also won the Nobel Prize in economics, came to the same conclusion – 'income itself does not provide a full summary of the anxiety facing individuals'[2]. Success is not just about economics. It is no use to be filthy rich if you are chocking in a polluted city, or – to be blunt – if the homicide rate is so high that you risk being shot.

So, we need a measure that takes into account all 'the anxiety' that Mr Stiglitz mentioned. This book outlines this in the form of the *Better Place Index* (or *BPI*), which takes into account, the environment, crime, health, education and, yes, economic well-being as well.

I already hear murmurs, and objections, What about religion? What about human flourishing? What about enjoyment of life? Well, of course, these are important things. But we need to sort out the basics before we get there. The American psychologist Abraham Maslow famously wrote a paper about what he called the hierarchy of needs. His basic idea was that you must satisfy your basics before you move on to consider the higher ones:

> If all the needs are unsatisfied, and the organism is then dominated by the physiological needs, all other needs may become simply non-existent or be pushed into the background. It is then fair to characterize the whole organism by saying simply that it is hungry, for consciousness is almost completely pre-empted by hunger. All capacities are put into the service of hunger-satisfaction, and the organization of these capacities is almost entirely determined by the one purpose of satisfying hunger[3].

2 Joseph Stiglitz et al. (2019) *Measuring What Counts*. New York: The New Press, p. 8.

3 Abraham Maslow (1943) 'A Theory of Human Motivation'. *Psychological Review*, 50(4), 370–396, at p. 373.

In this book, and the index developed in it, we deal with basic needs, because satisfying them is a prerequisite for doing things that gives meaning to life and makes it worth living. For as Maslow also wrote, 'the urge to write poetry, the desire to acquire an automobile, the interest in American history, the desire for a new pair of shoes are, in the extreme case, forgotten or become of secondary importance. For the man who is extremely and dangerously hungry, no other interests exist but food'[4].

But just measuring and ranking countries in the order they meet basic needs is not much use. Yes, of course, some will take comfort in being top of the list, and others may gleefully revel in *Schadenfreude*; pleasure derived from another country's misfortune. But this is really not that helpful.

But it might be asked, hasn't this been done already? After all, we live in an age of Big Data, and surely a list, and, indeed, a ranking of 'better places' must have been made, right? Well, not really, in fact. Not ones we can use anyway.

A quick look at the most widely cited indices will prove this point. The most commonly used is the *Human Development Index* compiled by the *United Nations Development Program* (UNDP)[5]. The problem with this index is that it uses other indices to create their own index, which is akin to creating averages out of yet other averages. Besides, this index is based on incomplete datasets for inequality.

Another index is OECDs *Better Life Index*. This is better in many ways, as it includes official data and surveys to measure well-being, the environment, material living condition and community engagement. But it only measures these for industrial countries, so it is far from complete[6].

The thinktank the *Legatum Institute* is another one. Their index, the so-called *Prosperity Index*, benchmarks 149 countries across categories such as personal safety, health and the environment[7]. In many ways, it is valuable, but it is based on many other indices, which makes it less than transparent. Further, the problem is that it includes values like freedom and democracy

4 Ibid. 374.

5 <http://hdr.undp.org/en/content/human-development-index-hdi>.

6 <http://www.oecdbetterlifeindex.org/#/1111111111>.

7 <https://li.com/reports/2019-legatum-prosperity-index/> Accessed 16 March 2020.

in the index. That is fair enough if you like democracy, but it means that you cannot use the index to test if democracy is good for prosperity. The index is, therefore, a bit biased, and, frankly, a bit circular.

The same is true for *The Worldwide Governance Indicators*, by the *World Bank*. This ranks countries with respect to six aspects of good governance: 'Voice and Accountability, Political Stability and Violence, Government Effectiveness, Rule of Law, Regulatory Quality, and Control of Corruption'[8]. But once again, these are not outputs all can agree on. They are factors that might be conducive to good governance[9]. So, to put it differently, we need a simple measure that allows us to rank countries using only factors that everyone can accept.

It is important to state at the outset that the BPI is not a measure of the 'best' society, just a better one, 'if men [and women] were angles, no government would be necessary'[10], wrote James Madison, one of America's Founding Fathers. But they are not. As the American statesman knew, we are dealing with human beings. This is not utopia, still less, heaven on earth. It is just a measure of which countries are 'better' – or worse – than others. And this, in turn, is just a measure to help us find out how we can make countries into 'better places'.

In Search of the Common Good?

To write about a 'better place' is nothing new. Since the dawn of civilisation, philosophers, writers and even some bookish rulers have come up with ideas of what is 'a good society'. For Saint Thomas Aquinas – a corpulent cleric whose reported size was only matched by his formidable

8 <https://info.worldbank.org/governance/wgi/>

9 It is beyond the scope of this book to provide a deep methodological critique of these measures. Interested readers should are encouraged Piero Stanig (2018) 'Considerations on the Method of Constructing Governance Indices', in Helmut K. Anheir, Matthias Haber and Mark A. Keyser (Editors) *Governance Indicators: Approaches, Progress, Promise*. Oxford: Oxford University Press, pp. 134–153.

10 James Madison (2003) [1787] 'Federalist Paper No. 51', in Alexander Hamilton, John Jay, and James Madison *The Federalist Papers*. New York: Signet Classics, p. 319.

intellect – the aim of law making was 'the ordering of the common good' – the *bonum commune*[11].

But what is that exactly? To begin with there are two types of answers. Some are 'utopians', they write books about the ideal world, as they see it, no matter how far-fetched this society might be. On the other hand, there are 'Realists', people who come up with what they consider to be practical blueprints for 'better' societies. The philosopher Jean-Jacques Rousseau, who inspired the French Revolution, wrote about 'men as they are and laws as they should be'[12]. He was a realist, whereas the ancient Greek philosopher Plato was a utopian. A former wrestler from a well-to-do family, he wrote a book called the *Republic*, which outlined the best imaginable world – as it happens ruled by philosopher-kings, suspiciously like the author himself.

When he later tried to put his ideas into practice as a political advisor in Syracuse, in present-day Italy, it was a complete disaster. Plato cut his losses and left dejected and despondent, 'principally through a feeling of shame with regard to myself, lest I might someday appear to myself wholly and solely a mere man of words'[13]. Once back in Athens, he wrote another book *The Laws*, which was more realistic – but also very tedious with drearily detailed practical recommendations on all sorts of minor administrative details, such as the regulation of the beggars in the marketplace and funeral procedures[14].

Yet, utopians have continued to write books. And some think that it is useful to have dreams as guiding lights. A writer recently suggested that utopias of the past have come true and that it is only by dreaming 'big' that we can get to the promised land[15].

Possibly so, but there are also things we wish did not come true. In the renaissance, that is 500 years ago, when Sir (later Saint) Thomas More

11 Thomas Aquinas (1959) 'Summa Theologica', in A. P. D'Entréves (Editor) *Selected Political Writings*. Oxford: Basil Blackwell, p. 111.

12 Jean-Jacques Rousseau (1964) 'Du Contrat Social', in *Jean-Jacques Rousseau: Œuvres completes*. Paris: Gallimard, pp. 951–1041, at pp. 347–524, at 351.

13 Plato (1997) 'Letter VII', in John Cooper (Editor) *Plato: Complete Works*. Indianapolis: Hackett, p. 1648.

14 Plato (1975) *The Laws*. Translated with an Introduction by Trevor J. Saunders. London: Penguin, p. 484 and p. 512.

15 Rutger Bregman (2018) *Utopia for Realists*. London: Bloomsbury.

coined the term 'Utopia' (it literally means 'no place'), he was not the only one to come up with an idea of paradise on earth.

In Thomas More's case utopia was rather tame, and certainly had some features, which some people today, would find appealing. For example, Sir Thomas wanted to ban fox hunting but legalise euthanasia – the latter is rather surprising given that he was later canonised as a Catholic saint[16]. But be that as it may, the fact of the matter is that his conclusions were rather liberal – not far from the average reader of *The Guardian* in the United Kingdom or *The Washington Post* in the USA. For example, Sir Thomas More also wanted higher salaries to workmen, 'coachmen, carpenters and farmhands, who never stop working', whereas he wanted the opposite for 'goldsmiths and money lenders, who either do no work at all, or do work that's not really essential'[17].

So, the problem with this utopia was – and is – that it is politically biased. Such thinking might provide inspiration, but it is almost inevitably prejudiced and represents one particular point of view. But inspiration is not a good thing in all cases. Sir Thomas was relatively modest – though even his ideas, as we just saw, are not shared by everyone today.

There were other utopias, which were more radical. A few years after More, an Italian Friar Tommaso Campanella wrote about the City of the Sun, where the wearing of high heels was punishable by death[18]. In the protestant world, the utopias were no less draconian. A less known Lutheran clergyman wrote about Wolfaria, a utopian society where there would be drowning of drunkards, public execution for adulterers, and beheading for anyone who taught any other prayers than the Lord's Prayer[19]. Utopias like this might be good for inspiring the Taliban, but they are unlikely to be cherished by everyone, and seem to be earlier versions of the dystopian societies described by novelist Margaret Atwood in the Handmaid's Tale[20] – or in

16 Thomas More (1965) *Utopia*. London: Penguin, Fox hunting p. 95 and euthanasia, p. 102.

17 More, *Utopia*, p. 129.

18 Tommaso Campanella (2008) [1602] *The City of the Sun*. Radford, VA: Wilder Publications, p. 23.

19 Susan Groag Bell (1967) 'Johan Eberlin von Günzburg's "Wolfaria": The First Protestant Utopia'. *Church History*, 36 (2), 122–139.

20 Margaret Atwood (2006) *The Handmaid's Tale*. London: Everyman.

the real life experiences described in The Gulag Archipelago, by the former political prisoner Aleksandr Solzhenitsyn, who lived through the system described by the Soviet leaders as 'actually existing socialism'.

So, the utopian approach is not necessarily much good when we are trying to find out what is 'a better place'. We need to find something – or rather some things – that everyone can agree on; both those who watch Fox News and the ones whose main source of information is CNN; the ones who read the New York Times, as well as those who rely on the Daily Telegraph.

Is such agreement possible? Some think not. Joseph A. Schumpeter, a celebrated Austrian economist and briefly a finance minister for his country, once famously, claimed that there is 'no such thing as a uniquely determined common good that all people would … be made to agree on by the force of rational argument'[21]. The same economist claimed to be 'the greatest economist in the world, the greatest horseman in Austria, and the greatest lover in all of Vienna'[22]. Nice line. Schumpeter was, by all accounts a humorous and entertaining chap. But that does not mean that his opinion should be accepted unquestionably; 'a witticism is not a rational proof'[23]. In fact, it seems rather uninspired and uncreative to say that we cannot agree on the common good, maybe in some abstract and philosophical sense. Of course, we do *not* all agree on whether equality s a bad thing, on whether the public sector should be large or small, or on immigration. But, as will be argued below, these are not really 'ends', rather they are 'means' to achieve them. The level of taxation, to take but one, is not a goal in itself, but a way to achieving higher welfare. For example, some people (those on the left) believe that higher taxes (within reason) will make society better.

21 Joseph A. Schumpters (1946) *Capitalism, Socialism and Democracy*. London: Unwin, p. 251.

22 Joseph Schumpeter quoted in Thomas K. McCraw (2007) *Prophet of Innovation: Joseph Schumpeter and Creative Destruction*. Cambridge, MA: Harvard University Press, p. 4. In fairness, Schumpeter said that he only became two of the three things. He never said which too, but remarked that there were many good horsemen in Austria.

23 Jean-Jacques Rousseau (1964) 'Considérations sur le gouvernement de Pologne', in *Jean-Jacques Rousseau: Œuvres completes*. Paris: Gallimard, pp. 951–1041, at p. 1007.

Those on the right believe that lower taxes (again within reason) are a means to creating a better society, and that higher taxes can lead to lower productivity, fewer incentives, and, consequently, lower welfare even for the poor.

We disagree on the means. That is what politics is about. But can we agree on common goals? And, if so, what are those objectives exactly? One way of answering that question is to use what we might call the 'anti-test'. This is a way to measure the things that it would be absurd to be against. For example, for all intents and purposes, everyone, regardless of religious beliefs or political persuasion, agrees that infant mortality is a bad thing; they are also against homicide and a polluted environment. And, at the risk of getting ahead of ourselves, these things can be measured, which brings us one step closer to identifying the 'better places', the ones that have 'success'. Let's look a little closer at the contenders for inclusion in a Better Place Index.

Nearly everybody in America is concerned about the large number of people who are murdered. The goal of a low homicide rate is a thing that unites all Americans – and folks in other countries too, we might add. The difference is not over the goal, rather what divides opinion is getting there. Film-maker Michael Moore – him of *Bowling for Columbine* fame[24] – believes that restrictions on the sale of handguns would solve the problem. The *National Rifle Association (NRA)* believes the opposite, and some even claim that more guns will lead to lower levels of crime[25]. But they share the goal; to lower the murder rate. So, we can add this to the list.

The same, is true for long life expectancy. Yes, of course, there are some who argue that we have a longing for death. Sigmund Freud, to name but one talked about a 'death drive'[26] – or a *Thanatos* as subsequent psychoanalysts

24 *Bowling for Columbine* was a political documentary, which explored the circumstances that lead to the 1999 Columbine High School massacre. The film was released in 2002.

25 J. R. Lott Jr (1999). 'More Guns, Less Crime: Understanding Crime and Gun'. *Southern Economic Journal*, 65(4), 978–981.

26 Sigmund Freud (1987) 'Beyond the Pleasure Principle' in *On Metapsychology*. Middlesex: Penguin, p. 316.

have called it[27]. And the German Romantic poet Novalis wrote *Sehnsucht nach dem Tode* – it would translate something like, 'longing for death',

> Into the bosom of the earth,
> Out of the Light's dominion,
> Death's pains are but a bursting forth,
> Sign of glad departure.
> Swift in the narrow little boat,
> Swift to the heavenly shore we float[28].

But Novalis is the odd one out; a kind of poet-version of rock stars with a death wish like Any Winehouse, Kurt Cobain, or Jim Morrison. For 99 percent of the population, a long life is a good measure of a good society.

What else do we need to add? An obvious candidate for inclusion, as noted, is low infant mortality. For who could possibly disagree with that goal? Surely, there is nothing more heart-breaking than children dying young, a life so promising cut short before it has properly begun. For this reason, we should have a low level of infant mortality as part of the index. In the United States, 55,000 children die before reaching their fifth birthday[29]. That *is* very sad. But on this we have seen improvements. Until 1,800 roughly one third – 33 percent – of all children died before the same age. But not all countries are this fortunate. In Ghana, which is *not* among the poorest countries in Africa, about six million children die before reaching this age[30], or 34 out of every 1,000 children. In America the figure is six for every one-thousand live births. To improve this number, is likewise a no-brainer.

27 Daniel Cho (2006) 'Thanatos and Civilization: Lacan, Marcuse, and the Death Drive'. *Policy Futures in Education*, 4(1), 18–30.

28 Georg Philipp Friedrich Freiherr von Hardenberg Novalis (1772–1801) Hinunter in der Erde Schoß/Weg aus des Lichtes Reichen/Der Schmerzen Wut und wilder Stoß/Ist froher Abfahrt Zeichen/Wir kommen in dem engen Kahn/ Geschwind am Himmelsufer an (Sehnsucht nach dem Tode, in Hymnen an die Nacht1800).

29 <https://www.ncbi.nlm.nih.gov/books/NBK220806/> Accessed 18 April 2020.

30 UN Inter-agency Group for Child Mortality Estimation (2013). Levels & Trends in Child Mortality – Report 2013. New York.

So too is increased wealth. Yes, it is true that GDP per Capita is a crude measure, and indeed one that sometimes creates perverse incentives. In a prescient, some might even say prophetic, speech Robert Kennedy (JFK's brother who was running for the Presidency in 1968) voiced this concern in a speech at *The University of Kansas* three months before he was assassinated:

> Gross National Product counts air pollution and cigarette advertising, and ambulances to clear our highways of carnage. It counts special locks for our doors and the jails for the people who break them. It counts the destruction of the redwood and the loss of our natural wonder in chaotic sprawl. It counts napalm and counts nuclear warheads and armored cars for the police to fight the riots in our cities. It counts Whitman's rifle and Speck's knife, and the television programs which glorify violence in order to sell toys to our children. Yet the gross national product does not allow for the health of our children, the quality of their education or the joy of their play. It does not include the beauty of our poetry or the strength of our marriages, the intelligence of our public debate or the integrity of our public officials. It measures neither our wit nor our courage, neither our wisdom nor our learning, neither our compassion nor our devotion to our country, it measures everything in short, except that which makes life worthwhile.

These words have not ceased to ring true. But, despite this, economic growth is still a valid goal. We might agree with the tenor of Kennedy's speech. Some might even agree with the sentiment, famously stated by the eighteenth-century writer Jean-Jacques Rousseau, that 'you must make money contemptible'[31]. At some abstract philosophical level, some might want to return to the state of nature and be a 'noble savage', as the same philosopher dreamed about. But as a practical political goal? No, not really! Just try to do the anti-test. 'Let's reduce average income!' This is not a rallying cry that would win many votes. The only one who has pursued this as a deliberate policy was the *Khmer Rouge* in Cambodia in the 1970s.

But Robert Kennedy still had a point that GDP is not the *only* measure. That is not controversial. This, in fact, is the reason for writing this book

31 *Jean-Jacques Rousseau: Political Writings*, Madison, WI: The University of Wisconsin Press, p. 225.

and for devising The Better Place Index. But to have a measure of a good society, a way of assessing economic wealth is necessary, and GDP (for all its short comings) is the only one we have at the moment. If a better one comes along, then, of course, we might use that. But for the time being, there is no alternative to GDP. So, we add that to the list too.

So far, then we have a low murder rate and a low infant mortality, as well as long life expectancy and a high GDP per Capita.

What else is there? Well, most people would also add education. And this is where it gets tricky. For here we are not comparing like with like. Some would say that reading and writing, say at the age of ten is a good measure. But reading Chinese – with thousands of signs – is more complex than reading English, Greek or Arabic. Moreover, we simply do not have global league tables of literacy rates. So, what can we do?

Other international indices, such as the United Nations' Development Programme's Human Development Index simply measures the years of schooling. This, certainly, is not an ideal way of gauging the quality of education. No less a writer than Thomas Hobbes, perhaps the greatest philosopher ever to write in the English language, was dismissive of this kind of quality-control. 'For', he wrote in his masterpiece *Leviathan*, 'it is possible [that] long study may increase and confirm erroneous sentences; and where men build on false grounds, the more they build the greater the ruin[32]'.

Certainly, Hobbes had a point. But, once again, we have to consider the alternative. Many years of study may equate with more years of indoctrination. Still, the anti-test again comes in handy. All other things being equal, most people would want many years of schooling as opposed to few. So, Hobbes' caveat notwithstanding, we can add years of education to the list. But, like GDP, it is not an ideal way of assessing the quality of education.

Statistics and Big Data are useful, but the problem is often that many important things do not lend themselves to quantitative analysis. That is just a fact of life. But, nonetheless, figures, data and numbers provide an invaluable starting point.

So far so good. So, what else should we include? The environment is an obvious candidate. After all, many people talk about the climate

32 Thomas Hobbes (1973) *Leviathan*. London: J. M. Dent & Sons, p. 143.

catastrophe. But this is where it becomes difficult. For many people – so-called *climate deniers* – question whether rises in global temperature are man-made, or just a result of the natural fluctuations which have always occurred. Should low CO_2 emissions be part of the Better Place Index?

Once again, notwithstanding the disagreement over the effects of climate change, even politicians who have opposed measures to cut greenhouse gasses, for example, US President Donald Trump – not a politician who is known for his enthusiastic pursuit of 'green' policies – sent his followers (and many beside them) the following *Tweet*:

> 'Which country has the largest carbon emission reduction? AMERICA! 91% of the world's population are exposed to air pollution above the World Health Organization's suggested level. NONE ARE IN THE U.S.A.!'[33]

In the interest of accuracy, the forty-fifth president of the United States was not entirely correct. In fact, the US only cut its emissions 12 percent[34]. France cut them by 20 percent, Britain by 29, and Denmark by 34 percent between 2000 and 2016[35]. This disinformation aside, the point here is that Trump also cared about this issue. To include CO_2 emissions per 100,000 inhabitants is not a sign of ideological bias. There is broad agreement about the goal. The difference is over policy and how to solve what is regarded (almost) by everyone as a problem.

So, we have a list of the issues that everybody – or practically all – believes to be important. Such near universal goals constitute what the American political philosopher John Rawls called an 'overlapping consensus', or things people can agree on despite 'considerable differences in [their] conceptions of justice'[36].

But how do we measure these? The reader will not be surprised to learn that statisticians have developed complex and mathematically difficult

33 <https://twitter.com/realDonaldTrump/status/1169356703126773762> (Accessed 12 March 2020).

34 <https://www.c2es.org/content/u-s-emissions/>

35 <https://www.factcheck.org/2019/09/trumps-false-facts-on-the-environment/> (Accessed 12 March 2020).

36 John Rawls (1971, 1999) *A Theory of Justice* (Revised Ed.). Harvard University Press, p. 340.

tools. These are certainly useful for highly specialised journals for experts, but they are not necessary to get the basic picture across.

What we are doing in this book is to 'democratise knowledge'. What we seek is to present an understandable number that ordinary people can use when they want to hold their leaders to account.

For the sake of developing this index, we hold that the following are positives that no one would disagree with[37]:

- Low CO_2 emissions (measures by tonnes per 100,000 people);
- Many years of education;
- Low homicide rate per 100,000;
- Low Infant mortality rate per 100,000;
- Long life expectancy;
- High GDP per Capita in Purchasing Power Parities.

These figures can be compared individually, as on a dashboard, but we believe they cannot be viewed in isolation. Politicians cannot be held to account for one figure, but for a full range of policies.

It is not enough to just lower crime, if health deteriorates and the economy is stagnant. So, we have developed a measure that measures them all together and give them all equal weight[38].

The calculations can be found in Appendix A at the end of this book. If you turn to this you will see that Switzerland comes out on top, followed by Luxembourg, Norway, Ireland and Sweden. With Germany in tenth Place and the UK in twelfth spot.

37 CO_2 Emissions data based on <http://www.globalcarbonatlas.org/en/CO2-emissions>; Years of education data taken from the Human Development Reports <http://hdr.undp.org/en/data>; Homicide data taken from <http://www.smallarmssurvey.org/tools/interactive-map-charts-on-armed-violence.html>. GDP, Infant Mortality, and Life Expectancy data taken from <https://data.worldbank.org/>

38 Statistically this is done using so-called Z-scores. Simply put, this is a way of *standardising* the scores for each of these factors, a way of using an average, and making the data comparable. The details of how this is calculated may not interest everyone, and we will not go through it here (Those interested in the details can consult the website <www.thebetterplaceindex.com>).

'In Switzerland, they had brotherly love, they had five hundred years of democracy and peace – and what did that produce? The Cuckoo Clock.' Thus, said Harry Lime (Orson Wells' character) said in the film *The Third Man*[39]. In fact, this clock wasn't even a Swiss creation. It was invented in the German state of Baden-Württemberg around 1740.

But what Switzerland has – apart from cheese, secret bank accounts, muesli, and army knives – is good government. The long-established Alpine republic is consistently the highest placed country on the Better Place Index. Other countries are doing well, too, of course, for example, the Scandinavian countries, Ireland, Luxembourg and Singapore. And other countries do abysmally year after year, for example, South Africa and El Salvador. It is tempting to start to look for patterns, but we will wait with that.

Let's first get an overview. We can basically divide the countries into categories. There is Switzerland, Luxembourg, Norway and Ireland, which are the only countries above 1.10. Behind these we have a few countries between 0.90 and 1.09, which includes Britain and Germany, in respectively, ninth and tenth place.

But we have to go rather far down before we find the United States in twenty-sixth place with a score of 0.71, just behind Slovenia, Cyprus and Canada.

Why is America so low relatively speaking? Mainly due to the high levels of crime, 'according to the *United Nations Demographic Yearbook*, the Japanese homicide rate per annum was six victims per million persons. Most of Western Europe had similar or slightly higher rates … The UN estimate for the United States was a whopping 98'[40]. The updated figures we used for this book find the same trend. In the USA 4.96 are killed per 100,000 every year, in Slovenia it is only 0.48 and in both Canada and in Cyprus it is 1.26. But America also scores lowly because infant mortality is relatively high. In Sweden only two out of every infant die at birth. In the USA the figure is six. Much lower, of course, than Afghanistan (48

39 This is of course paraphrasing Orson Welles, in the film *The Third Man*, directed by Carol Reed (1949).

40 Martin Daly (2017) *Killing the Competition: Economic Inequality and Homicide*: London: Routledge, p. 21

out of 100,000) and Angola (52 out of 100,000), but twice as high as in comparable countries like Austria and Australia.

Of course, it is not all doom and gloom for the USA. America is still in top thirty, mainly because it is a rich country. The thing is that USA would be higher up if we solely measure by GDP. But if we take all the other important factors into account, then things are not so rosy. America, the most powerful country in the world, is not among one of the top ten places to live.

America is still ahead the former communist countries in Eastern Europe, the likes of Slovakia and Croatia in the thirty-second and thirty-fifth place, and just ahead of Cuba in thirty-sixth place all of them with BPIs in the high 50s.

In fact, Cuba does well, mainly because it has long life expectancy, just below seventy-nine years, low infant mortality four out of every thousand live births (two points lower than the USA). The Communist led island nation also has roughly the same murder rate as the USA (just below five per hundred thousand). Of course, the Cubans aren't rich, compared to Americans, Brits and Australians. But with a GDP per Capita of $8,821, they are slightly richer than their neighbours in the Dominican Republic ($8,050), not far behind Brazil at just over $9,000 per year, and certainly considerably ahead of Ecuador at $6,000. Moreover, the Cubans have a low carbon footprint at three metric tons per person. So, it stands to reason that they are doing surprisingly well on the Better Place Index.

If we move further down the list, we have countries with a BPI in the 40s. These include Sri Lanka and Estonia, before we come to the countries in the 30s, like Lebanon and Costa Rica. And in the 20s, we have the likes of Uzbekistan and Kyrgyzstan (both with BPI: 0.25), Thailand (0.23) and, finally, China (0.22).

In the teens you have Algeria, Paraguay and Turkey. An aspiring member of the EU, the latter country is, in fact, not that successful. Perhaps surprisingly, its GDP per Capita is relatively low at $ 9,370; it has a relatively high infant mortality at 9.1 deaths per 1,000 live births, so there is certainly room for improvement, but so far that has not been the case. There was a more or less consistent fall in the BPI-score for Turkey until 2016, when it rose temporally only to be reversed again in 2018.

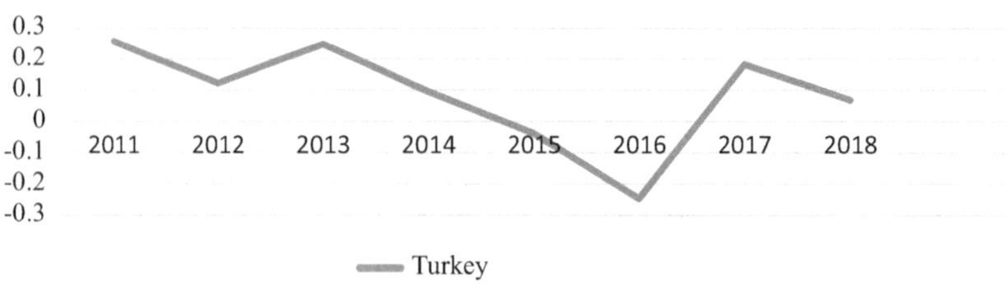

Figure 1.1 BPI Change in Turkey 2010–2018

What is perhaps equally interesting is that the countries on the Arab peninsula, the likes of Kuwait in 106th place and Saudi Arabia immediately below, are so low down on the index. This is unexpected, especially given their riches and low levels of crime. They both have a BPI-score of -0.09. But again, this is where the other factors come in. The two Arabic countries have an exceptionally high carbon footprint. Above all, Saudi Arabia and Kuwait score badly because of massive CO_2 emissions; 19 metric tons for the former and 26 metric tons for the latter. By contrast the similar figure for Germany in only 8 metric tons – although this country is the third largest exporter of goods behind China and USA. So, Saudi Arabia and Kuwait might be as rich as Spain, but their life expectancy (in both cases just below 75 years) is much lower than in the Southern European country on the Iberian Peninsula; the average life expectancy for a Spaniard is 83 years old.

In other words, there are countries which we perceive as successful on the global stage, but which are not – places that are international powers but whose citizens suffer from crime, low incomes and pollution, to name but three factors.

There has been much talk about the BRIC economies, an acronym for Brazil, Russia, India and China. These countries were much hyped when Economist Jim O'Neill, then the chairman of *Goldman Sachs Asset Management*, introduced the shorthand at the beginning of the Millennium[41]. They have even been referred to as the 'Big Four'.

But in terms of BPI, these countries are far from 'big' when it comes to being safe, rich and healthy. The four nations may be powerful militarily

41 Jim O'Neill (30 November 2001) 'Building Better BRICs' *Global Economics Paper* No. 66 Goldman Sachs & Co.

and, in some cases, even feared by their neighbours. But the people who live in them are not getting the benefit of this. Admittedly China and Russia (BPI: 0.13) are in Top 100 – though very far down– coming in at, respectively seventy-fifth and eighty-eighth place. India in 116th place has a negative score of – 0.14 and Brazil, two places below, scores only -0.15.

Of course, some people would argue that the actual number is only part of the story. What matters is if there is an improvement, or the opposite[42]. China, Russia, India and perhaps to a lesser degree Brazil did not have a favourable starting position, so they have a lot of catching up to do. Hence, it is better to look at the improvements. If, indeed, the countries did make improvements Brazil dropped by a relatively modest -0.02, Russia (despite a rapid increase after 2016) dropped by -0.6 overall in the period, and India saw a consistent drop of -0.11 over in the years since 2010. Prime Minister Modi's *Bharatiya Janata Party* (BJP), in power since 2013, have claimed that they were making India great again. Measured by BPI, they have not. Our figure has dropped while the Hindu-Nationalist party has been in power.

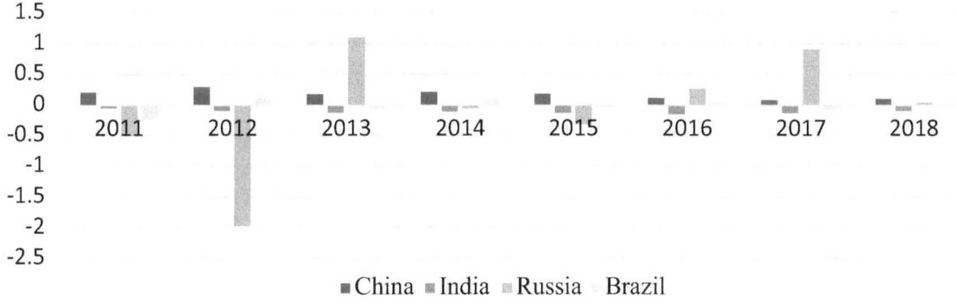

Figure 1.2 BPI Change in BRIC Countries 2011–2018

The same might not be said for China. Overall, this massive country had a net BPI increase of 0.16 over the period, but, as the Figure 1.3 shows, the performance is not that rosy on closer inspection. For all the talk about a more powerful China under the rule of Xi Jinping, there has been a consistent trop in the BPI-growth rate for the People's Republic since he came to power in 2012.

42 A complete list of changes in BPI can be found at <www.betterplaceindex.com>)

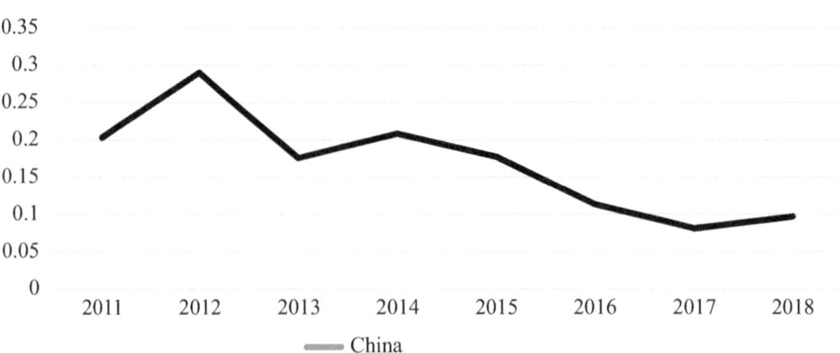

Figure 1.3 BPI Change China 2010–2018

As already said, these countries (for a number of external as well as self-inflicted, internal, historical reasons) started from a low base.

By contrast economies like Britain, France Germany, Japan, the USA – and smaller economies like Italy and Canada – (in short, the G7-countries) had a much more favourable starting position.

These nations had developed industries centuries earlier and – so some would argue – were able to exploit poorer parts of the world in the late nineteenth and early twentieth century when all but one of them had colonies in Asia and Africa.

So how have they fared recently? Overall, the G7 countries have done well, there has been a modest average growth overall, though only of 0.01. America has done best with a consistent growth averaging nearly 0.04. This is graphically represented in the Figure 1.4.

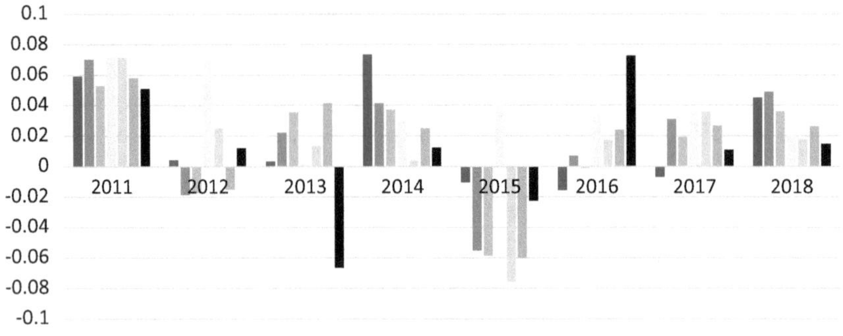

Figure 1.4 BPI Change in G7 Countries 2011–2018

The other G7 countries have had modest ups and downs. With an overall improvement of 0.02 Britain has an average growth similar to that of France and Germany (both 0.03), but her performance has been fluctuating, just like that of Japan. But in both cases the trend has been slightly upward bound as graph shows (Figure 1.5).

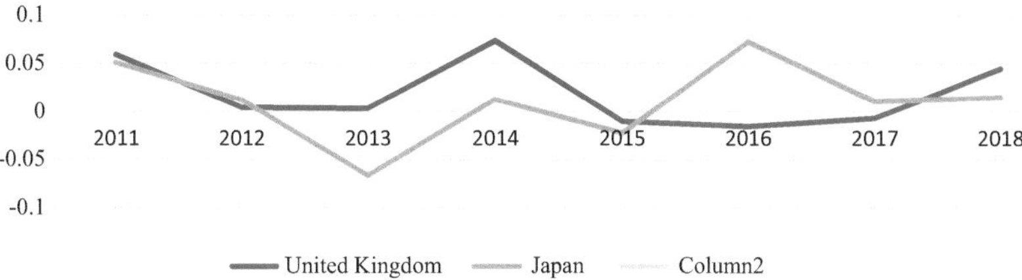

Figure 1.5 BPI Change: United Kingdom and Japan 2010–2018

It is tempting to attribute political and economic factors to these changes. For example, France improved after the election of Emmanuel Macron, America's average dropped slightly from 0.4 to 0.3 after Trump became president. Some will look for confirmation that Japanese Prime Minister Shinzo Abe's so-called *Abenomics* (it stands for increased money supply combined with increased government spending), has improved the country's standing. And some in the United Kingdom will notice that Britain immediately dropped into negative territory after the Brexit referendum in 2016. Others, perhaps of a different persuasion, will notice that the UK bounced back in 2018.

But these analyses are superficial, and in any case, premature. Social science is much too complex to draw simplistic conclusion. We need to look into each of the factors – and we will do so in the subsequent chapters. But before we do so, it is necessary to look at the countries that fare poorly.

It is probably not surprising that Zimbabwe is in 124th place with a BPI of -0.26. For example, on the day when this sentence is being written, a headline on the BBC website, read, 'Zimbabwe – once again on the brink of collapse'[43]. Things have certainly not been rosy for the impoverished and misruled African country. But it is probably unexpected that Jamaica

43 <https://www.bbc.co.uk/news/world-africa-53062503>. Accessed 18 June 2020.

(-0.28) is below Zimbabwe in 127th place. More commonly associated with Rum, Reggae and *Red Stripe Beer* than a low quality of life, Jamaica scores badly on the index, perhaps above all because the supposedly chilled island nation has a murder rate that is almost off the scales. Forty-four individuals per 100,000 people are murdered every year. This is second only to El Salvador at 52 per 100,000.

Why does Zimbabwe do better? For starters the African country is cleaner – 0.8 metric tons per head compared to Jamaica's 2.50. Zimbabwe is not a safe place, with a homicide rate of 6.67 (roughly like that of the USA), but this is far below the murder rate on the Caribbean Island. What is doubly tragic is that Jamaica *used to be* a peaceful place. When the country gained its independence in 1962, the murder rate was just below four in every one-hundred thousand inhabitants, just above that of present-day Switzerland. No wonder former Jamaican Prime Minister P. J. Patterson described, the murder epidemic, as 'a national challenge of unprecedented proportions'[44].

Other countries that are sometimes perceived as 'strong' also fare poorly. If Nigeria 'can get its socioeconomic act together, it may also be the continent's first superpower', wrote the American magazine *Newsweek* at the time when this index was being compiled[45]. Well, so far, the largest West-African country has spectacularly failed in this endeavour. It is currently in 169th place. Why is this so? It is not surprising, really, when we look at the figures; infant mortality is heart wrenchingly high in Nigeria (75.7 deaths per 1,000 live births), the homicide rate of 9.5 per 100,000 rate is almost twice that of the United States, and the average Nigerian lives for only just under fifty-three years. Add to this that its GDP per Capita is a mere $2,000 – and it matters little that the carbon footprint is a miniscule 0.55 metric tons per year for every individual. Nigeria is not doing well.

Without analysing each and every country it is sadly expected that the three of the four worst placed countries are war torn Yemen (-1.22),

44 P. J. Patterson quoted in *Washington Post*, 'Murder 'Madness' Bedevils Jamaica: Government Struggles to Curb Wave of Slayings and Address Underlying Causes', 27 July 1999; page A13.

45 Sam Hill (2020) 'Black China: Africa's First Superpower Is Coming Sooner Than You Think', Newsweek, 15 January.

Afghanistan (-1.26) and the Central African Republic (-1.43) – the fourth one is Lesotho. Civil wars kill many people, life expectancy goes down rapidly and the opportunities to produce goods and services are near to none existent. In the well-known phrase of Thomas Hobbes, 'no arts, no letters, no society; and which is worst of all, continual fear and danger of a violent death; and life of man [and woman] solitary, poor, nasty, brutish and mean'[46].

So, and this is the big question, when and why are countries successful? What drives success? A command economy under one-party rule has worked reasonably well in Cuba, but then again, others with the same sort of system have fared poorly, Venezuela for example. Some countries with very interventionist economic policies and high taxes have occasionally been successful, for example, in the case of Sweden. But to cherry-pick example is not a scientific way to answer this question. We must look at the matters systematically. We begin with the economic factors in the next chapter.

46 Thomas Hobbes (1973) *Leviathan*. Dent: London, 65.

CHAPTER 2

The Economics of a Better Place

It was the best of times for some. It was the worst of times for others. The stock market was booming, and investors were becoming filthy rich. But there was also anxiety. There had been mass immigration, and some of the immigrants belonged to a different religion, which created suspicion, as they tended to live in ghettoes. There was occasional violence, and 'some of the perpetrators of the heinous acts of terrorism were new immigrants … This fact allowed nativist elements within the United States to create periodic spasms of anti-immigrant hysteria'[1]. New technologies of instant communication meant that information was spreading quickly – and many, especially those living away from the larger metropolitan areas were feeling left behind. A new movement known as Populists were challenging the wealthy elite. One of their leaders, who was running for the presidency, summed up the grievance of many when he outlined his economic philosophy:

> There are two ideas of government. There are those who believe that if you just legislate to make the well-to-do prosperous, that their prosperity will leak through on those below. The Democratic idea has been that if you legislate to make the masses prosperous their prosperity will find its way up and through every class that rests upon it[2].

The reader could be forgiven for thinking this was an address delivered in the second decade of the twenty-first century. It wasn't. In fact, the speaker

1 Ernest G. Rigney and Timothy C. Lundy (2015) 'George Herbert Mead on Terrorism, Immigrants, and Social Settlements: A 1908 Letter to the Chicago Record Herald'. *The Journal of the Gilded Age and Progressive Era*, 14 (2), 160–172, p. 160.

2 William Jennings Bryan in Dickinson, Edward B. (1896). *Official Proceedings of the Democratic National Convention Logansport.,* Ind.: Wilson, Humphreys, and Co, p. 233.

was William Jennings Bryan, a Democrat who – unsuccessfully – ran for election in 1896. The period 1870–1900 was known as the *Gilded Age*, and it was characterised by immigration by Irish and Italian Catholics to the United States, growing economic inequality, the invention of the telephone and immense riches for the so-called *robber barons* – the likes of Cornelius Vanderbilt, John D. Rockefeller, and Henry Ford – who benefitted from the expansion of the new communication technologies, the railway and the emerging oil industry.

Hundred and twenty-five years on from Bryan, the philosophies of economics can still be divided into those who believe that increased wealth for the riches will trickle down to the less well-off, and those who take the opposite view.

In many ways, the story goes back further still, and can be associated with what is sometimes known as the doctrine of *laissez-faire*, made famous by the celebrated Scottish economist Adam Smith in his 1776 book *The Wealth of Nations* – though originally developed by earlier French economists, such as François Quesnay, Anne Robert Jacques Turgot, and other so-called *Physiocrats* who advocated a kind of agricultural capitalism. But while these thinkers are covered in textbooks, they are not generally known by the wider public, and, more importantly, they did not have Smith's turn of phrase. Much has been made of the Scotsman's observation that 'it is not from the benevolence of the butcher, the brewer, or the baker that we expect our dinner, but from their regard to their own interest. We address ourselves, not to their humanity but to their self-love, and never talk to them of our own necessities but of their advantages'[3]. And his perhaps even more celebrated observation, from later in the same book that 'he [the consumer or the capitalist] intends only his own gain, and as in many other cases, [he is] led by an invisible hand to promote an end which was no part of his intention'[4].

Smith's writings were used as ammunition for those who generally opposed state intervention; as confirmation of the view that the virtues of selfishness would lead to overall gain for all. 'Smith's book was', said

3 Adam Smith (1925) *The Wealth of Nations*, Vol. 1. London: Methuen & Co, p. 16.

4 Adam Smith, *Wealth of Nations*. Vol. I, p. 421.

an admiring economist, 'a stupendous palace erected upon the granite of self-interest.'[5]

Never mind that Smith was actually talking about foreign imports, and was quoted out of context, the metaphor of the invisible hand has been taken as affirmation that markets work best when left to themselves; that politicians and the state should leave the economics to the private sector. This was a revolutionary idea. In the middle ages, Saint Thomas Aquinas criticised speculation and the quest for riches, because it 'always implies a certain baseness, in that it has "not of itself any honest or necessary object". Seeking a profit was "not for its own sake", but "for the public welfare and to provide the country with the necessities of life"'[6]. Economists from other cultures, for example, from China, were equally shocked by this lack of planning. Upon visiting Washington in 1817, Jiang Youxian, an envoy to the Chinese Emperor – who described the Americans as 'Barbarians' – reported back to Beijing, that 'commercial affairs are managed independently by private individuals and these individuals are not controlled or deputed by the head man [the President]'[7]. Like Saint Thomas, the Chinese did not believe in the invisible hand.

So, who is right? Is economic life more prosperous when left alone? When we allow free reign for the supposed virtues of selfishness? Or are we richer, safer and better off when the public sector is there to lend a helping hand?

Previously, these different philosophies of economics could merely cite selective examples in support of their superiority. Certainly, narratives are powerful, and there is a case for using stories to illustrate a point, but there is always a danger of cherry-picking – of choosing the examples that *prove* that our pet theories are right. What we need is to look at the

5 George Stigler, 'Smith's Travels on the Ship of State', in Andrew Skinner and Thomas Wilson (Editors) *Essays on Adam Smith*, eds. (Oxford: Clarendon, 1975), p. 237.

6 Thomas Aquinas (1959) *Summa Theologica*, Questio LXXXVII. Oxford: Clarendon, p. 173.

7 Jiang Youxian quoted in Yuezhi Xiong (2002) 'Difficulties in Comprehension and Differences in Expression: Interpreting American Democracy in the Late Qing'. *Late Imperial China*, 23(1), 1–27, at p. 2.

big picture. And for this, statistics is useful. So, to get started, let's take a concrete example, namely taxation.

One of the differences between the two philosophies is over the role of taxes. Those who believe in *laissez-faire* or 'trickle-down economics' fear that high taxes will kill economic incentive and that lower taxes will kick-start the economy. David Ricardo, a free market economist writing in 1817, found that 'the best in taxes is that which is least'[8]. Economists of the same persuasion have echoed this sentiment, 'reducing the burden which government places on the economy ... tax cuts, is the surest way to promote growth. I have never heard of a country that taxed itself into prosperity'[9], claimed Arthur Laffer, an American economist who advised Ronald Reagan and who went on to counsel Donald Trump on economic matters.

Others, typically on the other side of the argument, say the opposite. Paul Krugman, a *New York Times* columnist, who also happens to have won the *Nobel Prize* for economics, described a proposal to raise income tax for the richest to 70 percent as 'fully in line with serious economic research'[10].

So, the positions are uncompromising; one favours tax cuts – the other does the opposite. What do we do? Statistics provide an answer. You probably all remember Coordinate Systems – or Cartesian Co-ordinates, as they are called if you are fancy. Basically, it is just a simple scatterplot of the type you see every day. One way of testing if taxes make countries richer or poorer is to draw a graph. So, let's do that. Figure 2.1 shows the relationship between the marginal tax rates in different countries (that is the highest bracket of income taxation) on the vertical axis and the average GDP per Capita on the horizontal line.

8 David Ricardo (1932) [1817] 'The Principles of Political Economy and Taxation' in Pierro Sraffa (eds), *The Works and Correspondence of David Ricardo.* Vol. I. Cambridge: Cambridge University Press, p. 159.

9 Arthus Laffer in *The Spectator*, <https://www.spectator.co.uk/article/how-to-kick-start-the-economy>, Accessed 11 June 2020.

10 Paul Krugman (2019) 'The Economics of Soaking the Rich', *The New York Times*, 5 January 2019. A more scientific article that says the same is Diamond, P., & Saez, E. (2011). 'The Case for a Progressive Tax: From Basic Research to Policy Recommendations. *Journal of Economic Perspectives, 25*(4), 165–190.

If you eyeball the graph, you can probably see that there is a tendency that higher taxes are associated with a higher GDP per Capita. Basically, the more tax you pay, the richer the country is. Now, eyesight being what it is – and mine isn't good – such graphics cannot be trusted entirely. Luckily there is a statistical technique that can measure the relationship between two variables. It is called the 'Pearson's correlation coefficient'. This measure is used all the time in statistical analyses of everything from liver diseases research to the strategies developed by *Liverpool Football Club* (the Scouse soccer team has pioneered the use of sports statistics). We will use this technique for the rest of the book, so you better get used to it! And it is rather neat. So, let's get the basics out of the way. How does it work? Overall, the correlation can be between 0 percent (no correlation at all) to 100 percent (perfect correlation).

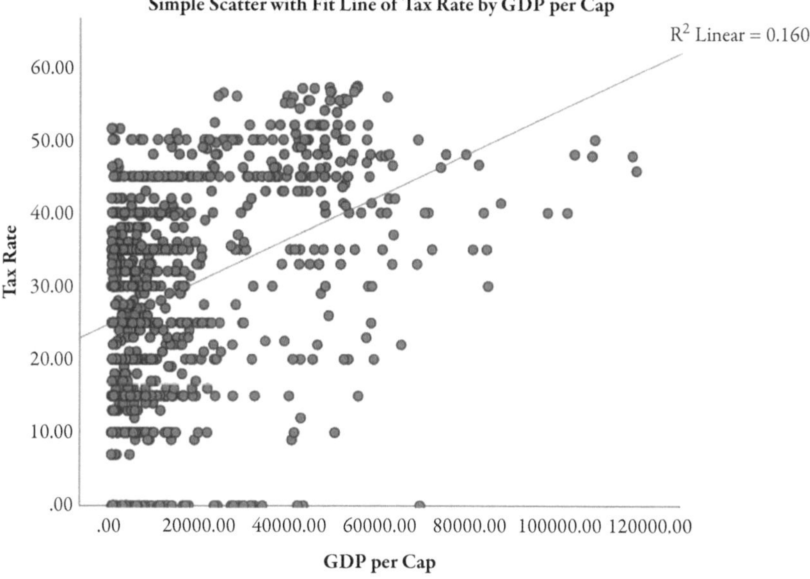

Figure 2.1 Tax Rate and GDP per Capita

The numbers can also be -100 – which means a perfect negative correlation. Now the world being what it is, we never have a perfect statistical relationship, but it is commonly agreed that a correlation of over fifty is a *very* strong correlation, that a correlation between thirty and forty-nine is a medium correlation and that one between twenty and twenty-nine is a small correlation[11]. Anything below that is normally disregarded. In academic textbooks it is a bit more complicated, but for all intents and purposes, it is a bit like percentages.

To measure the statistical relationship between the tax rate and the GDP per Capita we can use this technique. The graph seems to suggest that there is appositive relationship between higher taxes and more economic wealth, but is that really so? Yes, it is! When we do the calculation (which can be done on a smartphone) we get a correlation of forty, with a margin of error of less than one percent. So, the evidence does suggest that there is a case for higher taxes to increase overall wealth. It is not surprising when you think about it really.

Taxes give money to the public sector, which can be used to kick-start the economy. If money is left to the wealthy, they might just squander it in yachts or space travel. If the money is spent by the public sector, it can be targeted to certain sectors in times of need. This might not be welcome news for those who believe in trickle-down economics. And, they might argue that a correlation does not establish a fact. After all, there is a correlation between the number of people that drown in swimming pools per year and the number of films American actor Nicolas Cage stared in, and this correlation is even stronger at forty-eight (See the Table 2.1).

But there is a difference. For starters we have a very small number of cases, and this means that we have a very high margin of error – in this case plus/minus 15 percent. This is too much for serious analysis. We don't know if the correlation is actually fifteen percent lower or fifteen percent higher. And, as a general rule of thumb, statisticians never accept a margin of error of more than 10 percent to either side. In this book, by the way, we only accept a margin of error of one percent. We are dealing with important issues and we want to treat politics as an exact science because *Big Data* allows us to do precisely that!

11 This is based on Cohen, J. (1988) *Statistical Power Analysis for the Social Sciences,* 2nd edn. Hillsdale, NJ: Lawrence Erlbaum Associates, pp. 79–81.

Table 2.1. Nicolas Cage Starring Roles and Number of People Drowning in Swimming Pools. *Sources: Centres for Disease Control and Prevention and IMDB*

	1999	200C	2001	2002	2003	2004	2005	2006	2007	2008	2009	
Number people who drowned by falling into a swimming-pool Deaths (US) (CDC)	109	102	102	98	85	95	96	98	123	94	102	
Number of films Nicolas Cage appeared in Films (IMDB)	2	2	2	3	1	1	2	3	4	1	4	

But, more importantly, every statistical correlation must be backed up by a credible story, and by examples that prove the statistical association. Do we have that for the relationship between taxes and wealth? Yes, contrary to what Arthur Laffer said, economic history provides evidence aplenty of this correlation. For example, John Kenneth Galbraith, one of the most prominent economists in the twentieth century, pointed out that 'the American economy had one of its highest rates of growth, its highest levels of employment and in some years a substantial budget surplus in the period immediately following World War II, when the marginal rates on the personal income tax were at a record level'[12].

So far so good, but, as we discussed in the previous chapter GDP per Capita only tells part of the story. What we are interested in here is general well-being, and we measure this by the Better Place Index. What happens if we correlate the marginal tax rate with BPI? Again, it is useful to start with a graphic representation.

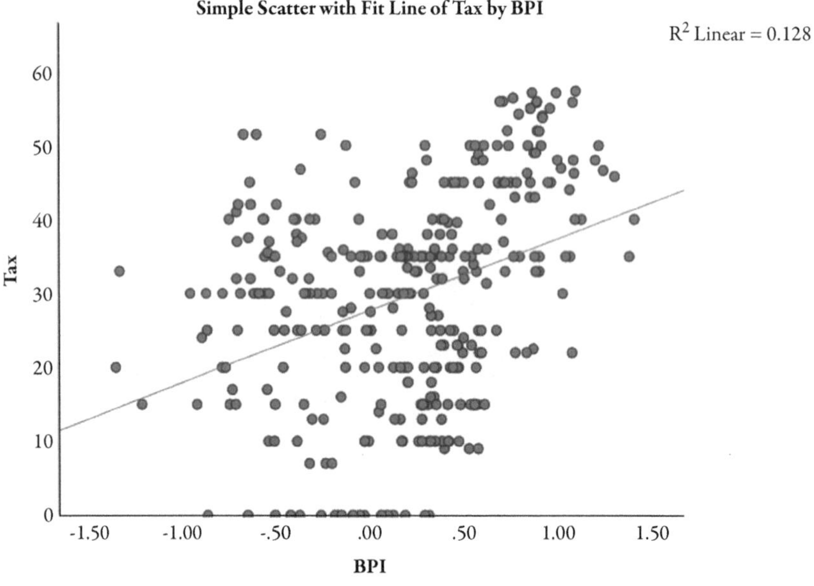

Figure 2.2 Tax and BPI

12 John Kenneth Galbraith (1996) *The Good Society: The Humane Agenda*. Boston: Houghton Mifflin Company, p. 65.

Eyeballing the graph seems to confirm the same pattern as we saw for the relationship between higher income tax and GDP per Capita. In this case, we have to admit that the relationship is a little bit smaller. The correlation is thirty-six. But this is still a reasonable association, and certainly one that goes against the view that higher taxes mean lower productivity – and with that everything else. The idea that economic output will go south as people have to pay more money to the taxman, and that taxes create a disincentive to work, innovate and invest, is not supported by the numbers. In many ways, it is the other way around.

In fact, quite a lot of things improve when taxes increase, including health. Statistically speaking you add 0.17 years to your life for every extra penny in the pound you pay in taxes. Not, needless to say, because giving more to the taxman somehow mysteriously makes you healthier but because some of this money is spent on improving the health system. Generally speaking, and of course there are exceptions (USA being one of them), health spending is correlated with higher taxes (there is a correlation of forty between the two). In the same way, there is a positive relationship between education and taxation. In terms of pure numbers, one percent tax increase adds an extra year to the average education of a child.

It is almost as if all good things go together – though many might not generally regard taxes a positive. Thus, there is even a small statistical tendency that higher taxes reduce the level of CO_2 emissions. One of the reasons, though it is probably too early to tell, would suggest that countries with relatively high taxes spend more on environmental Research and Development. For example, Luxembourg, with a marginal tax rate of just over 45 percent, spend about four percent of the total expenditure on R&D on environmental technology, whereas the USA where the taxman only takes 37 percent allocated less than one percent to this[13].

So far, we have only looked at the levels of taxation. The evidence is pretty clear that higher taxes has a number of positive benefits; the higher the taxes the higher GDP per Capita, and, though, at a marginally lower level, the more you pay in tax the higher the score on the Better Place Index.

13 The OECD (2014) 'Environmentally Related R&D' <https://www.oecd-ilibrary.org/docserver/9789264235199-21-en.pdf?expires=1592320534&id=id&accname=guest&checksum=7E507ACB36BE87C1237FC7772184A432> Accessed 16 June 2020.

Adam Smith, though often depicted as a tax-cutting crusader and prophet of the minimal-state, never shared the view that taxes should be miniscule. Rather he believed that 'the subject of every state ought to contribute towards the support of government, as nearly as possible, in proportion to their respective abilities'[14]. It was almost as if Smith was saying, 'from each according to his ability to each according to his needs', but the man who wrote these words was not, of course, Adam Smith, but a certain Karl Marx[15].

The recommendation following from this seems clear, higher taxes – while perhaps never popular – improve general welfare. But does this mean that the economic philosophy associated with this is consequently correct?

The Size of the State

In the 1930s, the Cambridge economist John Maynard Keynes famously proposed that running a deficit on the public accounts made sense in times of economic downturn. Previously it had been taken as granted that governments would save in times of economic recession. 'They shouldn't,' Keynes argued. They should do the opposite. They should spend money to increase demand. If you build a bridge, the workers would get paid, and they would create employment for the publican, who in turn would make more money which he could spend on a new car, which would create work for the factory workers, and so on. 'The additional wages and other incomes paid out are spent on additional purchases, which in turn lead to further employment,' Keynes wrote[16]. He called this the 'multiplier-effect', and argued that even squandering money would create demand, and hence jobs and wealth[17]. This paradox was not welcomed by all. Least of all industrialists. His

14 Adam Smith (1925) *The Wealth of Nations*, Vol. II. London: Methuen & Co, p. 310.

15 Karl Marx (1972) *Critique of the Gotha Programme*. Moscow: Foreign Languages Press, p. 17.

16 John Maynard Keynes (1933) *The Means to Prosperity*. London: Macmillan, p. 10.

17 Keynes, *Means to Prosperity*, p.12.

views shocked orthodox sensibilities, then and now. The ideas that consumption is the goal of economic life, that savings could be pathological, that public-sector deficits are necessary and virtuous in a slump, that interest rates should be kept low have always conflicted with respectable banker and business views. Yet the Depression and World War II appeared to prove him right[18].

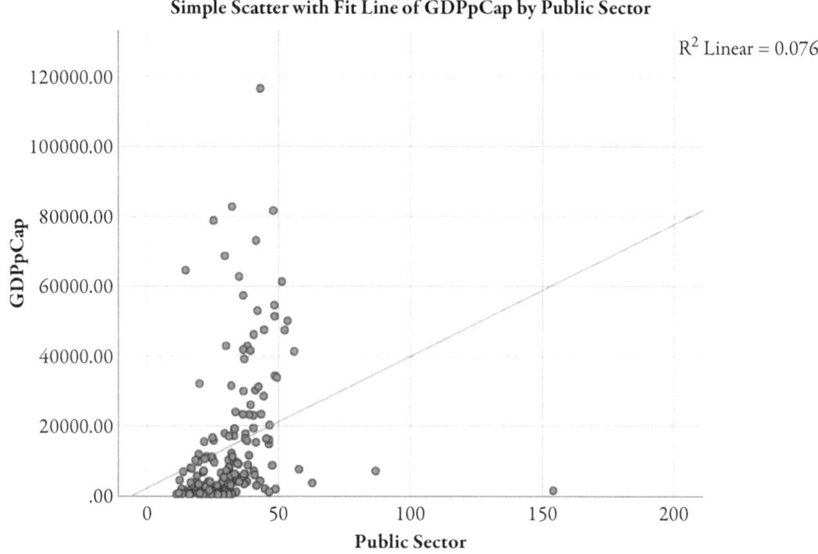

Figure 2.3 GDP per Capita and the Size of the Public Sector

His view was out of fashion for several decades after the 1970s. But, in more recent years, economists have rediscovered Keynes – though not all of them have admitted it. For example, Japanese Prime Minister Shinzō Abe has practised what has been called 'Abenomics', which involves public investment even if this will lead to budget deficits[19], and in the wake of both the financial crisis in 2008 and during and after the Corona Pandemic in

18 John Kenneth Galbraith (2009) 'John Maymard Keynes', in Wiley Online Library, <https://onlinelibrary.wiley.com/doi/full/10.1002/9781118474396.wbept0560>, Accessed 12 June 2020.

19 Though to be fair, Abenomics, consists of the 'three arrows' of monetary easing, financial stimulus and structural reform.

2020 even conservative governments pushed through policies modelled on the ideas of Keynes.

Others have been less enamoured by his ideas. Milton Friedman, an American economist who came to represent the backlash against the Englishman, bluntly stated that, his book (it was Keynes' 1936 tome *The General Theory of Employment, Interest and Money*[20]) had 'contributed substantially to the proliferation of overgrown governments, increasingly concerned with every aspect of the daily lives of their citizens'[21].

So, according to Friedman's *critique* it all comes down to the size of the public sector. The larger the part of the economy controlled by the government, the less room there is for private initiative and enterprise and hence, despite all the good intentions, everything stagnates. That is the argument anyway. But is it correct? There is little evidence for Friedman's gloomy view. While the correlation is not perfect, there is a statistical association, between a larger public sector and a higher GDP (the correlation is twenty-five). Admittedly, the correlation is small, but it is there and it goes against the view of Friedman's postulate. The idea that a large public sector leads to negative growth is simply not supported by statistics.

When David Ricardo wrote that 'the very best plans of finance is to spend little'[22], he was not basing this on data or anything as inconvenient as evidence. Maybe because he knew he was wrong, or possibly because statistics as a discipline had not been developed in the early 1800s. In any case, we now know that, at least statistically speaking[23], for every one percent increase in the size of the public sector, the average citizen earns another $376. But, of course, Ricardo was only talking about economics. What about general well-being? The environment? Health? Education?

When we look at the size of the public sector and education, we find that the two are positively related (The correlation is a medium thirty-six).

20 John Maynard Keynes (1936) *The General Theory of Employment, Interest and Money*. London: Macmillan.

21 Milton Friedman (1986) 'Keynes's Political Legacy', in *Keynes's General Theory: Fifty Years On*. London: Institute of Economic Affairs, pp. 45–55, at 45.

22 David Ricardo, 'The Principles of Political Economy and Taxation', p. 159.

23 This is based on a so-called regression analysis. This is a bit technical, so the keen reader should consult the 'refresher' published by *Harvard Business Review*. <https://hbr.org/2015/11/a-refresher-on-regression-analysis>

In pure statistical terms for every one percent increase in the public sector's share of GDP, children get 0.7 more years of schooling. The same is true for life expectancy. For this too we get a correlation of 36 percent. And, in numerical terms, a one percent increase in the size of the public sector adds 0.2 years to your life. It might not seem much, still, these things add up. Thus, the Swedes with a marginal tax rate of 56 percent on average live for eighty-three years.

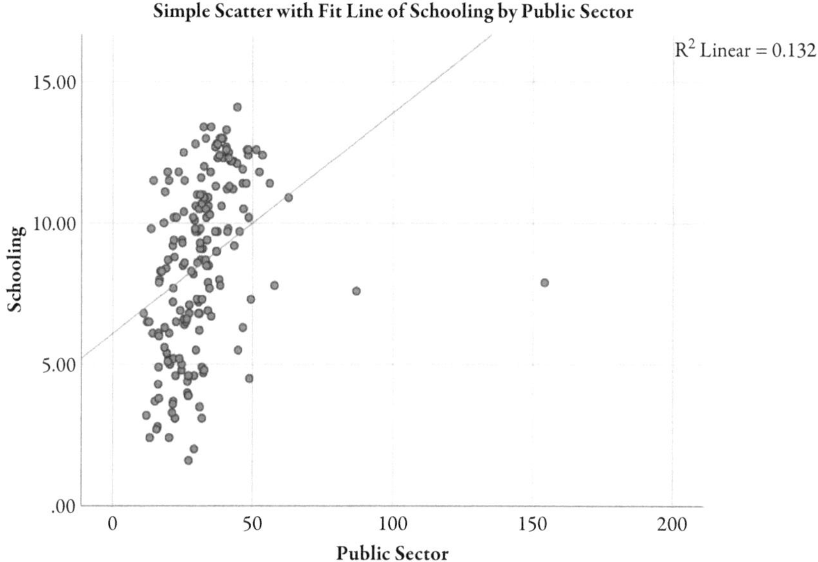

Figure 2.4 Years of Schooling and the Size of the Public Sector

By contrast, just across the Baltic Sea, the Latvians only pay 35 percent, but also – on average – have lives that are ten years shorter. Again, this is not as if by magic. It is not that a large public sector automatically translates into longer lives. Needless to say, it has something to do with policies, with implementation of these, and with political will. Still, it is noteworthy that people who live in countries with larger than average public sectors don't just live longer, but that these countries also have more doctors per thousand people. The graph (Figure 2.6) vividly illustrates this relationship, namely the over 50 percent correlation between the number of doctors and the size of the public sector.

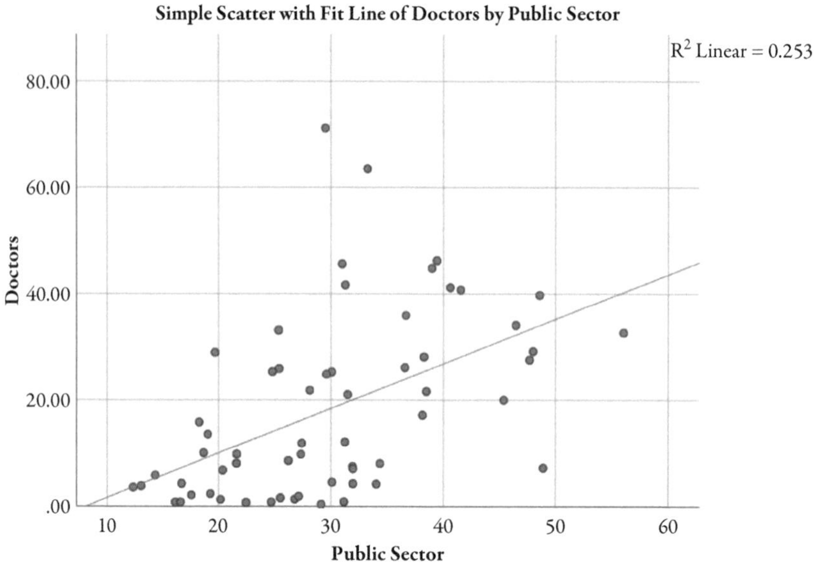

Figure 2.5 Number of Doctors and the Size of the Public Sector

However, not everyone will agree. Some might argue that the proportion if the GDP accounted for by the public sector is a bit too crude a measure. Certainly, it can be finessed. For example, and this might sound a bit technical, a case could be made that we should look at another measure known as General Government Final Consumption. This is defined as 'expenditure incurred by government in its production of non-market final goods and services', for example, spending on collective consumption (defence, justice and so on.) which benefit society as a whole, expenditures for individual consumption (health care, housing, education, that benefit people as individuals). What happens when we use this more refined measure? In general, the same. While the correlations are a little bit lower, the same tendency is there. While life expectancy, schooling and GDP per Capita are just below the 20 percent threshold, there is no suggestion that the negative assumptions regarding a large public sector are supported by the numbers. And there is still a correlation between Government Final Consumption and the number of doctors of thirty, and an even stronger correlation this number and hospital beds, in the latter case the association is thirty-two.

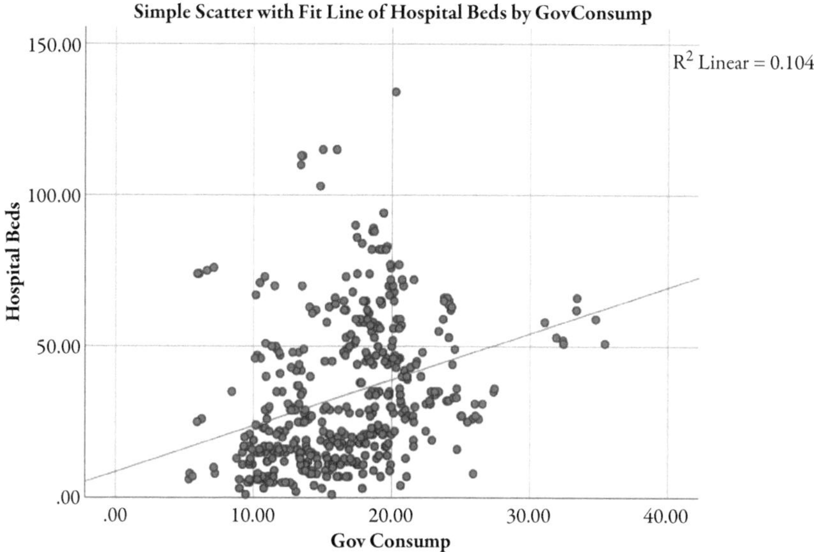

Figure 2.6 Hospital Beds and Government Consumption

This relationship, of course, is dependent upon political will, and democratic decisions. You can raise as much money as you like, but what really matter is how politicians (and ultimately the voters) decide to spend the money. This leads us inevitably to the question of politics. Could it be that some countries do better (or worse) because the underlying political preferences among the citizens (and their political parties), to put it bluntly, are bad for the economy?

Left or Right?

It's the Economy Stupid! So read a post-it-note placed over all the desks on Bill Clinton's presidential campaign in 1992. The then Governor of

Arkansas was a newcomer to Federal US politics, but he sensed that the only way to beat incumbent George Bush Sr. was by focusing on bread and butter issues, in short 'the economy'. Or, rather so he had been told in *focus groups* and in specially commissioned opinion polls, which he and his staff of political consultants pioneered. It was a massive success. Clinton Won. It worked, though, subsequent elections have shown that voters sometimes have other concerns than monetary ones, and that so-called *identity politics* can trump (admitted, pun intended) pocketbook issues, but that is for another day ....

The more interesting story, at least for the present purposes, was that Clinton, a liberal and a Democrat, was able to convince the voters that the economy was safe with him. Generally speaking, very few parties of the left have been able to win elections based on their claim to economic competence. Opinion polls have shown that more people trust the Conservatives to steer the economy[24].

The question is if this is warranted. Admittedly, this is very difficult to test statistically. But we can have a go. Over the past three decades researchers at *the WZB Berlin Social Science Center*, have coded election manifestos for parties in democratic countries. It is known as the *Manifesto Project*. Using a 0–100 scale, they have categorised political parties according to their ideology. Thus, a party on the far left, like the Communist Party, will get a score close to zero, whereas a party on the far-right, say like *Alternative für Deutschland* (AfD) will be close to a hundred. By taking an average of the scores of all the parties in a country we can categorise it as being either on the right or on the left. Thus, Sweden with a score of forty-five is slightly more *socialist*, whereas the United Kingdom was more *conservative* with a score of fifty-eight.

Obviously, such measures have to be taken with more than a pinch of salt. Still, it is interesting what it might reveal. Like in the previous cases, a graphic illustration is a good starting point (see Figure 2.7). So, here we go.

24 Reuter 'Conservatives more trusted on economy', 14 December 2009.

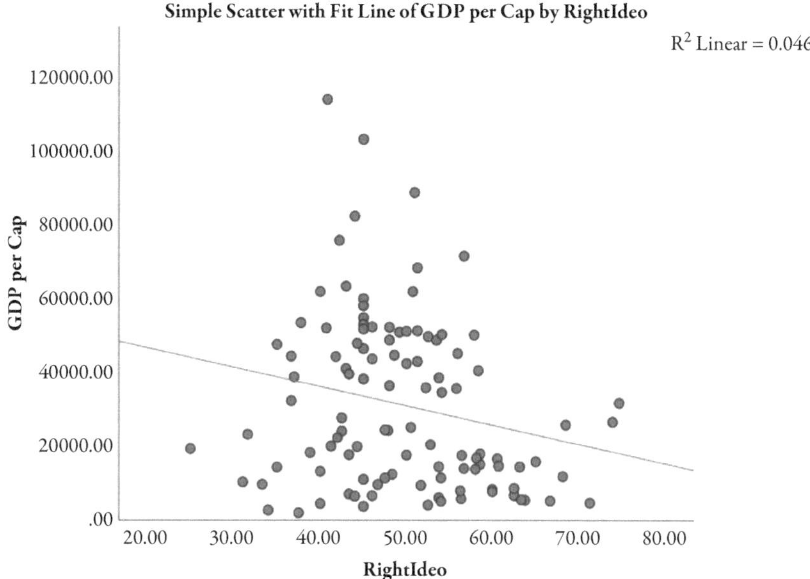

Figure 2.7 Right-Wing Ideology and GDP per Capita

Contrary to public opinion countries with a more left-leaning average on the political spectrum, as measured by the Manifesto Project index, do better. There is a negative correlation between GDP per Capita and a political system leaning to the right. Admittedly, the correlation is not overwhelming the correlation is only twenty-two, and it is based on a smaller number of cases as undemocratic countries are not generally included. When we do the same for the better place index, however, we do not get a statistically significant result. So, not everything is determined by ideology – as we shall explore in more detail below.

The surprising finding is that having a political system that leans to the left is good for the economy, but the ideological bend of a country has less of an impact on the overall well-being of a country. While there is a positive statistical relationship between left-ideology and a high score on the Better Place Index, this is only 13 percent way below the twenty mark threshold, and, in any case, the margin of error is over 15 percent – so in reality could be either 28 or -2.

The reason for this is that not all the factors that make up the Better Place Index are affected by ideology. Much as parties on the right like to claim that they stand for law and order, there is no correlation between ideology and the homicide rate. Nor is there a statistically significant relationship between life expectancy and ideology. On the other hand, those on the left often claim to be greener. Based on the statistical evidence, they are not. There is *no* correlation between ideology and CO_2 emissions.

So, in terms of scoring high on the Better Place Index, so far only high taxes and being on the centre-left is likely to have a positive effect on the economy. While there is no statistically significant association between ideology and inflation, there is a considerable correlation between unemployment and right-wing ideology. The figure is 36 percent (As Figure 2.8 shows).

It would seem that the claims that the centre-left are 'bad' for the economy are difficult to sustain in the light of the numbers.

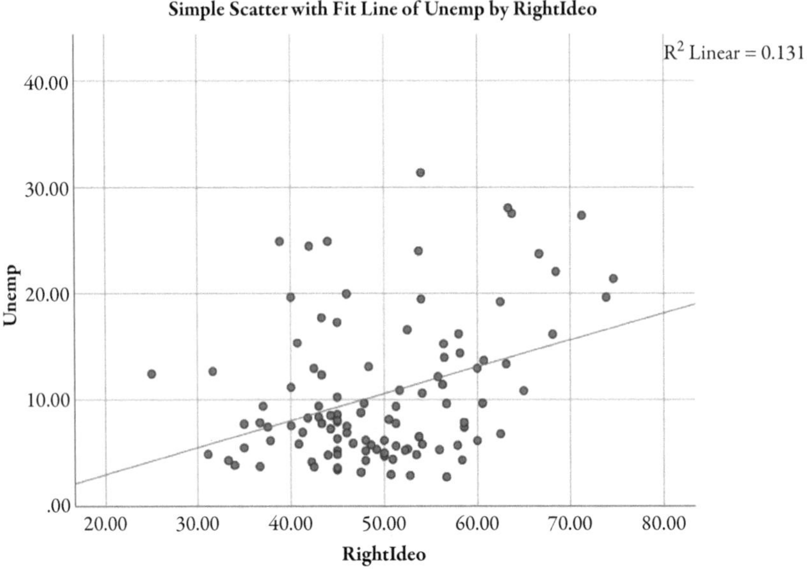

Figure 2.8 Unemployment and Right-Wing Ideology

In the case of Bill Clinton in America, this proved to be correct. Consistent with the philosophy of William Jennings Bryan a hundred years earlier, Clinton raised taxes, and the economy prospered. During his time in office, *all* the economic indicators showed improvement; there was growth of around four percent per year, job creation of a record 22.7 million. For the first time since 1969 there was a surplus for the federal budget in 1998 to 2001, when Clinton left office. When George Bush Jr took over, the taxes for the wealthy were immediately cut. And, the deficit grew once again. The economy was only revived after the election of Barack Obama, who used *the American Recovery and Reinvestment Act of 2009* to stimulate the economy by very much following the Keynes playbook. Obama increased taxes for the wealthiest, thus reversing the tax cuts enacted under his Republican predecessor. In line with the orthodoxy of Democrat thinking going back to Bryan, Obama lowered taxes for the poorer. The net result of his policies, a total of 11.6 million private sector jobs were created under his presidency. In the last thirty-six months of his term in office alone 8.1 million jobs were created. This number fell under Donald Trump, when only 6.6 million new jobs were created; a decrease of 19 percent[25].

One of the most pressing problems facing Obama was inequality. From 1950 to 1979, the top one percent earned roughly a ten percent share of pre-tax income. This had risen to 24 percent by 2007[26]. But, was this really a problem?

Inequality

'You do need some inequality to generate growth,' said French economist Thomas Piketty, a writer normally associated with the opposite view[27].

25 <https://www.nytimes.com/2019/08/27/opinion/trump-obama-economy.html>. Accessed 18 June 2020.

26 <http://inequalityforall.com/resources/#/>

27 Thomas Piketty in Globe and Mail 9 May 2014, <https://www.theglobeandmail.com/report-on-business/economy/fixing-capitalisms-growth-pains/article18586580/>. Accessed 12 June 2020.

The idea that inequalities spur people on to make an effort is a common trope in what is known as neoclassical economics. Friedrich Hayek, Margaret Thatcher's favourite economist, bluntly stated that 'even major scale inequalities may be of great assistance to the progress of all'[28], and he went on to state,

> 'Recent European experience strongly confirms this. The rapidity with which rich societies have become static, if not stagnant, through egalitarian policies, while impoverished but highly competitive countries have become very dynamic and progressive, has been one of the most conspicuous features of the post-war period'[29].

So, inequality, according to this view, makes people work harder. Status anxiety means that we don't want to fall behind, and hence, a certain level of inequality spurs people on. At least in theory. As a result of this, so the argument goes, there will be overall growth, and everybody will be better off if there is a modicum of inequality. Even if inequalities may seem grossly unfair, they can be – and ought to be – accepted if they 'can be arranged so that they are to the greatest benefit of the least advantaged members of society'[30]. Hayek's view is that they can.

It was rather different for the classic sociological and philosophical writers. Alexis de Tocqueville, a French nobleman who travelled in the United States two centuries ago took the opposite view. During his stay, in was in 1831, nothing struck him 'more forcibly than the equality of social conditions'. And, he reasoned, because of this equality, 'the majority of citizens will enjoy a greater degree of prosperity and the people will seem peaceful not because they have abandoned the hope of better things but because they know they are better off'[31].

Once again, we have an economic question, where opinion is divided. And once again, we can respond by statistics. Inequality is measured by a

28 Friedrich A. von Hayek (1960) *The Constitution of Liberty*. London: Routledge, p. 48.

29 Hayek, *The Constitution of Liberty*, p. 49.

30 John Rawls (1971) *A Theory of Justice*. Cambridge, MA: Harvard University Press, p. 266.

31 Alexis de Tocqueville (2003) *Democracy in America*. London: Penguin, p. 11 & 19.

number called the GINI-coefficient. Maximum equality is 0 and maximum inequality is 100. Like in all cases, it is not a perfect measure, but it is the only one we got, and is widely used.

So, first of all, are we better off if there is a significant degree of inequality? If we were to believe Hayek and the neoliberals, we would expect a rising curve as more inequality, according to their theory, leads to a higher GDP per Capita, and we would also expect a higher BPI.

However, this is not what the evidence shows, rather, more inequality equals a low economic output per person, and more inequality leads to a lower BPI. The countries that have a GINI Index of more than forty (that is countries like Brazil, Bulgaria, USA, Turkey and Venezuela) have an average GDP per Capita of 7,755 US Dollars per Year, and an average BPI-score of -0.10.

Conversely, the countries with a GINI index of less than forty (which include the United Kingdom, Belgium, Japan, Austria and Canada) have a BPI average of 0.40 and an average GDP per Capita of 14,911 US Dollars.

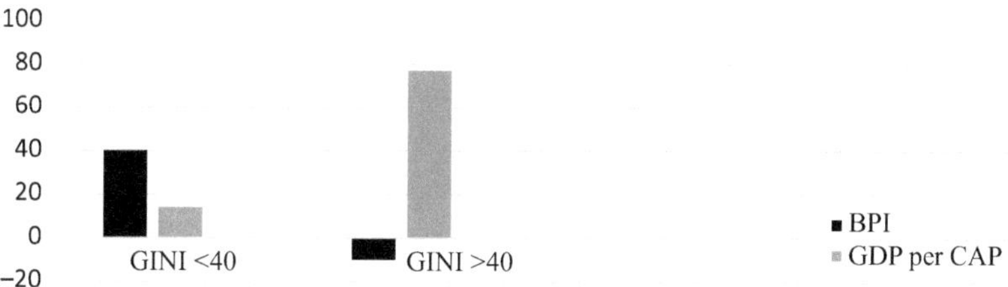

Figure 2.9 Inequality and BPI and GDP per Capita

Note: GDP per Capita in 1,000 US Dollars

This negative relationship between, respectively, GDP and BPI, and, on the other hand, inequality, are even more visible if we plot them on a graph.

If you don't trust the numbers, the calculation proves the same point. There is a negative correlation between high inequality and a high GDP per Capita (the correlation is thirty-eight). It seems that the argument developed by the classical economists is, simply not supported by data.

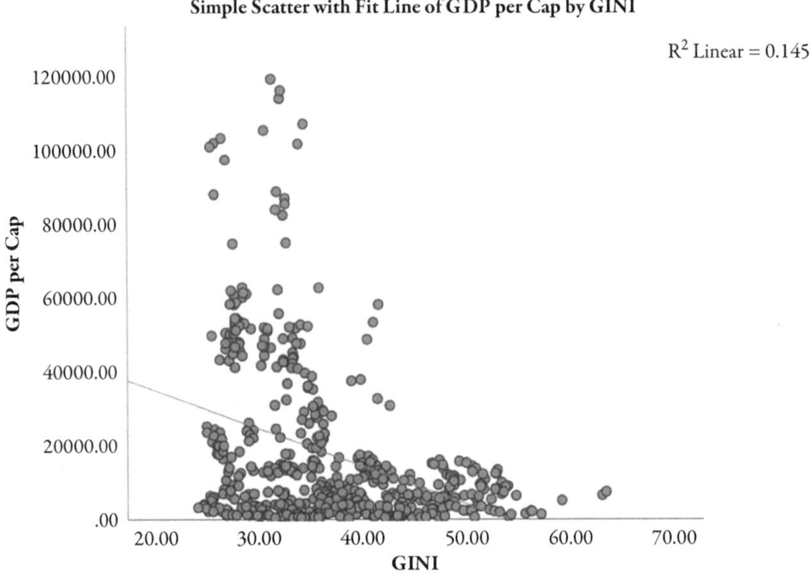

Figure 2.10 GINI Inequality and GDP per Capita

This might come as a surprise to many, even those you do not barricade under the neoliberal banner. But it is not a new revelation, nor one that runs counter to expert opinion. Branko Milanovic, an expert associated with the *International Monetary Fund*, likewise found that 'the empirical work conducted in the past twenty years has failed to uncover a positive relationship between inequality and growth'[32]. The data reported here allow us to go a step further. Here we find that there is a negative relationship between the two, that more inequality leads to lower economic output.

But, in this book we are not only interested in economic growth, we are interested in overall well-being as measure by the Better Place Index. So, then, what is the relationship between inequality and BPI? The answer is that the negative link between inequality and economic output is even stronger when we correlate the GINI Index with our measure. In fact, we find a very strong negative relationship between inequality and the Better Place Index (the correlation is -52).

32 <https://braveneweurope.com/branko-milanovic-why-inequality-matters> (Accessed 15 June 2020).

Contrary to all the hype about inequality propagated by the *New Right*, it seems that almost everything gets better if countries are equal. For example, there are more doctors in more equal societies (a correlation of forty-four). Likewise, there is also a positive correlation between the number of hospital beds per 1,000 people and equality. The correlation is a whopping fifty-nine.

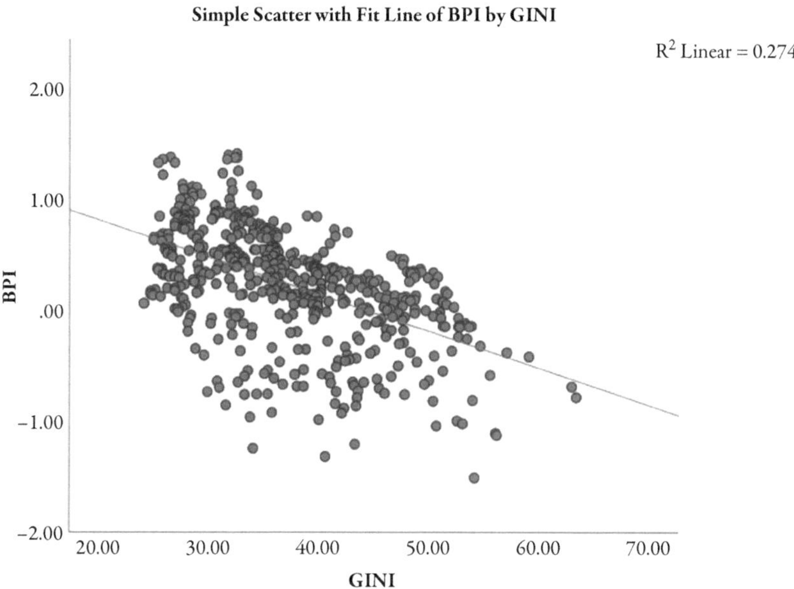

Figure 2.11 BPI and GINI Inequality

Further, there are fewer homicides in equal societies. Until the early 2000s this link had not been proved[33]. It has now. Criminologists have found clear evidence that 'income inequality is positively associated with crime rates'. According to an article in *Scientific American*, 'where financial disparities are greatest, the murder rate tends to be high', and the same article went on to say, 'Income inequality can cause all kinds of problems

33 M. B. Chamlin and J. K. Cochran (2006) 'Economic Inequality, Legitimacy, and Cross-National Homicide Rates'. *Homicide Studies*, *10*(4), 231–252.

across the economic spectrum—but perhaps the most frightening is homicide. Inequality—the gap between a society's richest and poorest—predicts murder rates better than any other variable.'[34] The calculations in this book, therefore, are not revolutionary. In fact, they are rather mainstream, but they may not be known to the public at large. They ought to be.

But, once again, the finer points need to be analysed using interviews and other qualitative data, that is techniques that can probe into the behavioural motivations. What the researchers found was largely sociological (and we shall have more to say about this in the next chapter). So, why are there more murders in economically unequal societies. An article summarising the most recent research explained it thus:

> The murders most associated with inequality, it seems, are driven by a perceived lack of respect. Like most killings, these are mostly perpetrated by males – and in societies with low inequality, there tend to be very few murders. To an outsider, these deaths, which make up more than a third of the homicides with known motives reported to the FBI, seem senseless: a guy looks at someone else the wrong way, makes a disrespectful remark, or is believed to have winked at another man's wife or girlfriend. These incidents seem too trivial to be matters of life and death. [For] a prosperous guy like me, if someone [insults me] in a bar, I can roll my eyes and leave. But if it's your local bar, you are unemployed or underemployed, and your only source of status and self-respect is your standing in the neighbourhood, turning the other cheek looks weak, and everyone soon knows you are an easy mark[35].

So, the evidence is pretty clear. And scary. For every one percent increase in the GINI index of inequality the homicide rate goes up by one. Inequality kills. Literally.

Social and economic inequality is not merely a matter of fairness, rather it is a matter of life and death. The relationship is not merely abstract, nor just a statistical association. As this example shows, there is a well-supported theory that explains the behavioural reasons why certain socially deprived victims of inequality react. To understand all, is *not* to

34 Maia Szalavitz (2018) 'Income Inequality's Most Disturbing Side Effect: Homicide', *Scientific American* 1 November <https://www.scientificamerican.com/article/income-inequalitys-most-disturbing-side-effect-homicide/> Accessed 17 June 2020.

35 Szalavitz, 'Income Inequality's Most Disturbing Side Effect: Homicide', *ibid*

forgive all. The behaviour of certain individuals – such as the males cited in the criminological research – should be condemned by all regardless of political persuasion. But outrage is no response to social and political problems. Rather, we must tackle the causes, and homicide is to a large degree a result of economic inequality. Those who (rightly) are appalled by criminal behaviour should start by addressing (and by reducing) economic disparities.

That inequality has negative effects on public health, economics and the crime rate is thus well documented and further substantiated by the date in this book. But that is not all. There is also a correlation between more inequality and more CO_2 emissions. Here the correlation is 43 percent.

That inequality is correlated with more CO_2 pollution could, of course, be one of those spurious coincidences, just like the case of Nicolas Cage and people drowning in swimming pools. The research shows otherwise. There are several country studies that record the same tendency. For example, in Turkey, 'deterioration in income distribution … reduce[d] environmental quality' and in China scientists found that 'that household carbon emissions increase with income inequality'[36].

So, we cannot claim this association between inequality and more CO_2 emissions as a new discovery. As far back as the 1990s, when the debate about climate change started in earnest, a scientist published a paper with the telling title, 'Inequality as a cause of environmental degradation'[37]. The explanation in the paper was that the wealthier in an unequal society basically prefer weaker environmental protection policies because they reap disproportionate gains from pollution. As the concern about these two problems have heated up, there has, predictably, been more research. One line of argument, based on more sociological reasoning, suggest that

36 See respectively, C. Demir, R. Cergibozan and A. Gök (2019) 'Income Inequality and CO_2 Emissions: Empirical Evidence from Turkey'. *Energy & Environment*, 30, 444–461.

Yulin Liu, Min Zhang, and Rujia Liu (2020) 'The Impact of Income Inequality on Carbon Emissions in China: A Household-Level Analysis'. *Sustainability*, 12(7), 1–22, at p. 18.

37 James K. Boyce (1994) 'Inequality as a Cause of Environmental Degradation'. *Ecological Economics*, 11(3), 169–178.

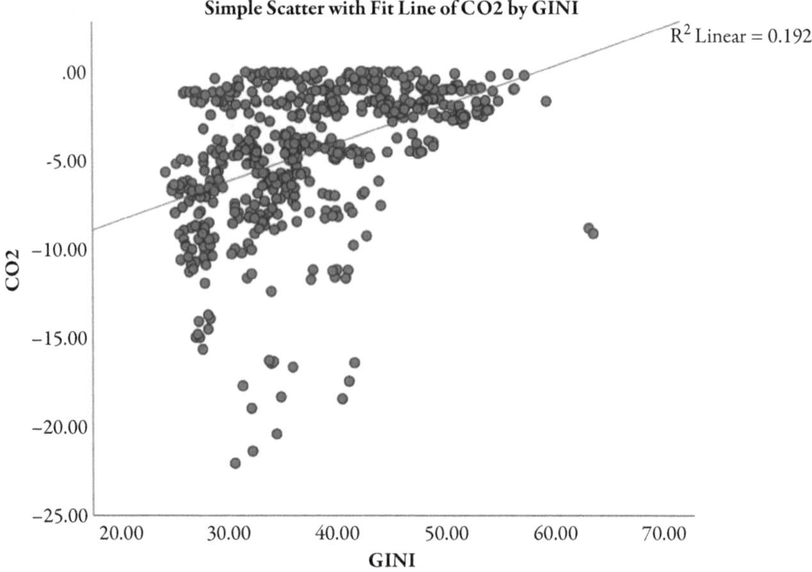

Figure 2.12 CO_2 Emissions and GINI Inequality

pollution is associated with status anxiety, thus in an unequal society, people do not want to be seen as poor. For this reason, so runs one argument, the wealthy, as well as the poor will engage in expensive and conspicuous consumption to maintain or obtain a higher social status[38].

That more equality is an almost universal panacea naturally begs the question what can be done to make societies more equal, as this in turn will improve their ranking on the Better Place Index.

So, what would make societies more equal? Maybe higher taxes for the rich would lead to less inequality? Or, perhaps, this would merely lead to an exodus of the wealthy, as was the case when France increased the income taxes in the early 2010s[39]. Statistically, there is a slight tendency that higher taxes lead to lower inequality, but the relationship is below the 20 percent

38 Schor, Juliet B. (1998) *The Overspent American: When Buying Becomes You*. Basic Books.

39 <https://www.france24.com/en/20150808-france-wealthy-flee-high-taxes-les-echos-figures>. Accessed 2 June 2020.

threshold, and cannot be regarded as proven. Another possibility could be that a large public sector leads to lower inequality. There is a statistical tendency in that direction. For every one percent increase in the size of the public sector (as a percentage of GDP) inequality falls by 0.3 percent. Not a massive correlation but enough to be reckoned with when you add up the numbers.

But the factors that really have an impact on inequality are institutional, procedural and legal factors. Researchers at the *University of Chicago* have developed a measure of *Due Process* and another one for the *Rule of Law*. In both cases, these are strongly associated with equality. The more things are done in accordance with rules – the more countries play by the book – the more likely they are to have economic equality – and with this the whole array of positive factors that go with it.

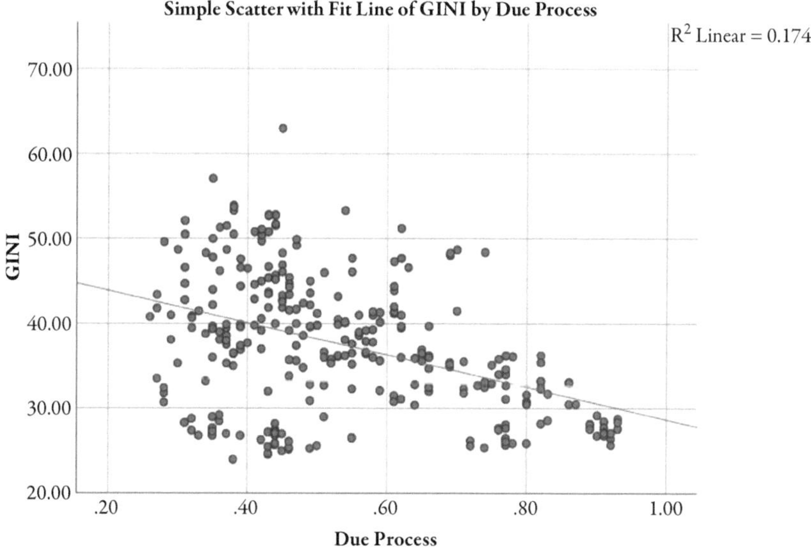

Figure 2.13 GINI Inequality and Due Process

Equality before the law – translate into equality of economic outcome. Statistically speaking there is a considerable negative correlation between due process and GINI inequality of -41.

But what else can be done? Perhaps, equality is correlated with education. The graph seems to suggest as much (Figure 2.14).

And this is borne out by statistics. There is a strong negative correlation between inequality and the average years of schooling of just over 51 percent.

This should probably not come as a surprise. And it is consistent with research, which shows that the more people are educated, the more likely they are to get a well-paid job. And, the better the remuneration, the less unequal the person. It follows, then, that the longer many individuals go to school, the less unequal the society as a whole tends to be[40]. This is another thing political leaders could easily deal with. By providing educational opportunities for the many, and not just for the select few, the less unequal the country would be, and this in turn, would alleviate a number of problems, from environmental disaster through to more hospital beds, to lower homicide rates and more economic prosperity.

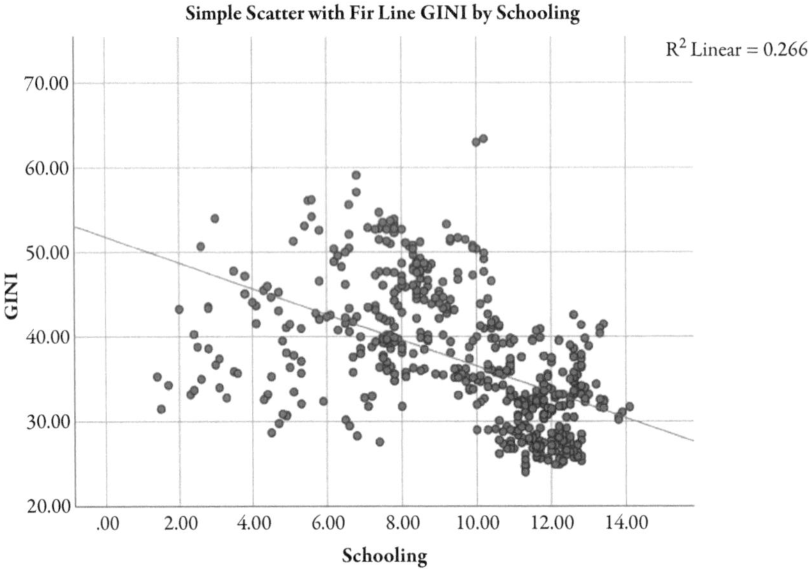

Figure 2.14 GINI Inequality and Schooling

40 Herbert Intis (2000) 'Does Schooling Raise Earnings by Making People Smarter?' in K. Arrow, S. Bowles, and S. N. Durlauf (Editors.) *Meritocracy and Economic Inequality*. Princeton, NJ: Princeton University Press, p. 118.

Another possibility is that inequalities are caused by more fundamental political problems. It is interesting that countries with presidential systems – such as the United States, Mexico and Turkey – are very unequal whereas the opposite is true for countries where the government is formed by the largest group in parliament. Statistically speaking, having a parliamentary system on average subtracts two points of the inequality index, whereas having a presidential system adds seven point to it. The reason for this could be that presidential systems often are characterised by gridlock when presidents disagree with a majority of the members of Congress. This means that policies to alleviate poverty – and inequality – are less likely to get enacted under this system than under a constitution in which Parliament reigns supreme. But to get into the nitty-gritty of this we need to look more closely into political institutions in general, but perhaps most important of all, we need to look at the relationship between democracy and the better place.

But before turning away from economics, it is useful to sum up what we have found. The basic lesson from this chapter is the more taxation, a larger public sector and lower levels of inequality are conducive to a high score on the Better Place Index – as well as a high GDP per Capita.

Consistent with that – but slightly more controversially – there is also a tendency that countries that are more left-leaning ideologically do better economically, though not on other indicators such as the environment or crime.

Of course, we have not analysed all possible economic systems. For better or for worse, all countries in the World (with the possible exception of North Korea) are capitalist economies. Free enterprise exists to greater or lesser degree. And before drawing the conclusion that more state intervention, a larger sector and higher taxes will lead to improvements, it is perhaps worth pointing out that the capitalist economic system (albeit in a regulated form), generally has improved general welfare for the many. After the Second World War, an economist who was sympathetic to socialism wrote that the superiority of the capitalist system did not 'consist in more silk stockings for queens but in bringing them within reach of factory girls in return for steadily decreasing amounts of effort'[41]. While 'capitalism in

41 Schumpeter, *Capitalism, Socialism and Democracy*, p. 67.

its original eighteenth- and nineteenth-century design was a cruel system', this was reformed into one that allowed for a larger role for the state – even when this meant higher taxes. The conclusion based on the economic data in this chapter does not support any radical policies or its overthrow. Rather the conclusion seems to be that the system of free enterprise should return to an earlier incarnation, one that does not see state intervention and higher taxes as a threat to capitalism, but rather one that acknowledges the public sector as a benevolent helper. This does not amount to socialism in its traditional sense. Rather, the conclusion appears to be much closer to policies that have been advocated by Christian Democratic Parties in Western Europe after the Second World War. One of the most successful economies there was the Federal Republic of Germany – to this day – a country governed by a Centre-Right Chancellor and with a relatively high tax rate of 45 percent.

The economic philosophy governing this country during its recovery was formulated shortly after the end of the Second World War by Konrad Adenauer – the first Chancellor of West Germany. The 'social market economy', he said,

> stands in stark contrast to the so-called free enterprise economy of liberal hue. To avoid a relapse into the 'free enterprise economy', monopolies must be independently controlled in order to ensure performance-based competition. After all, just as the state or semi-public agencies must not guide the industrial economy and individual markets, private persons and private associations must not assume such guiding functions, either. The social market economy refrains from attempts to plan and guide production, the workforce, or sales, but it does support planned efforts to influence the economy through the organic means of a comprehensive economic policy coupled with flexible adaptation to market studies. Effectively combining monetary, credit, trade, customs, tax, investment, and social policies, as well as other measures, this type of economic policy creates an economy that serves the welfare and needs of the entire population, thereby fulfilling its ultimate goal. Naturally, it must also adequately meet the needs of those parts of the population suffering hardship[42].

42 The CDU and the 'Social Market Economy': Düsseldorf Guidelines for Economic Policy, Agricultural Policy, Social Policy, and Housing (15 July 1949). Retrieved from <https://ghdi.ghi-dc.org/sub_document.cfm?document_id=3094>

The statistical analysis and the facts in this chapter do not call for more radical policies than the ones summed up by the main centre-right party in Germany in the early 1950s.

All this leads me to recount this personal anecdote. In 2009, yours truly was at the EU Council Meeting in Brussel. After German Chancellor Angela Merkel's press conference, the journalists ran off to file their copy, and the writer of this book was face to face with the most powerful politician in Europe. The EU had just consented to massive state interventions – which would increase public spending and increase taxes. Not, it would seem, the kind of policies espoused by a conservative politician like Frau Merkel.

'So, Frau *Bundeskanzlerin*, are we all Social Democrats now?' I asked.

Mrs Merkel slightly smiled, and answered politely,

> We want as much free enterprise as possible, and as much state intervention as necessary.

The German Chancellor's conclusion is perhaps a bit too pragmatic for those who prefer clear and unambiguous ideological statements, but it is rather in line with the conclusions of this chapter.

CHAPTER 3

The Sociology of a Better Place

Allah desires your well-being not your discomfort

Quran 2.185

'Men are more vigorous in cold climates,'[1] wrote the French sociologist Charles de Montesquieu. In addition to being a writer, the French nobleman was also a wine merchant. So, he travelled a lot. And, on his travels, he noticed that countries in the north were richer. Those in southern Europe and North Africa, by contrast, were poorer. And he concluded, that the warm climate made people lazy, whereas the colder climate in, for example, the Netherlands and Scotland, encouraged people to be more industrious, so that they could keep warm[2], 'in cold countries, one will have little sensitivity to pleasures ... in hot countries, sensitivity will be extreme'. Hence, the Scots, the Scandinavians and so on, would be dull and boring and get on with things, as there is little else to do, whereas those in the south would succumb to a pleasurable life. Much of what Montesquieu said was, to be honest, based on some rather pseudo-scientific ideas that appear almost embarrassing today. Classical writers were not always paragons of timeless wisdom. For example, the Frenchman believed that 'the strength of fibres in northern people cause them to draw the thickest juices from their food'[3]. We may laugh at his rather homespun biological theories.

1 Charles de Montesquieu (1989) 'De L'esprit des Lois', in Roger Caillpis (Editor) *Montesquieu: Œuvres Complètes*. Paris: Gallimard, p. 475.

2 Charles de Montesquieu (1989) *The Spirit of the Laws*. Cambridge: Cambridge University Press, pp. 231ff.

3 Montesquieu, *The Spirit of the Laws*, p. 232.

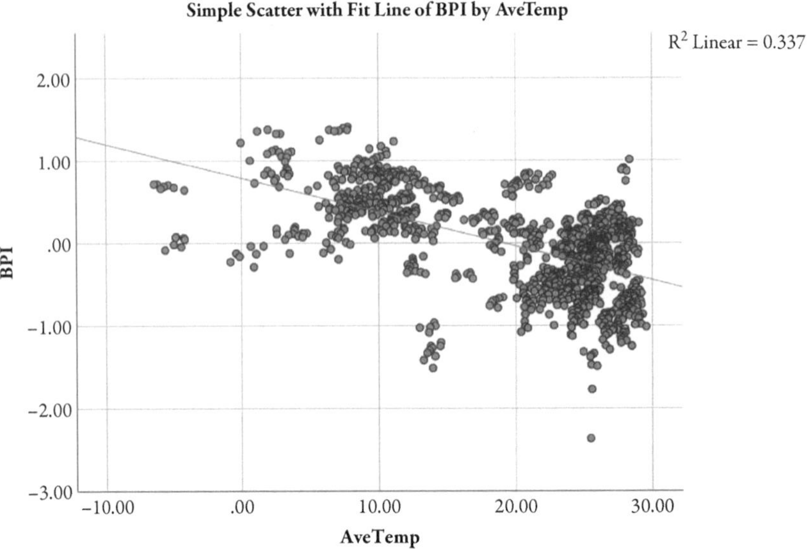

Figure 3.1 BPI and Average Temperature

Yet it is still conceivable that he could be right about the correlation between the weather and general well-being and wealth. Once again, the best way to ascertain this is to check the facts. And it seems that Montesquieu, had a point. At least there is a negative correlation between the average temperature and the BPI-Index of 58 percent. Basically, the colder the better, as the graph (Figure 3.1) also seems to indicate.

Montesquieu was not a racist – he even poked fun at the theories justifying slavery in his day. He did not subscribe to the view that certain groups were inferior. No, it was all to do with the weather, or rather the temperature. People in India, were, he said, 'without courage'. But not because they were of a different race, for, he went on, 'even children of Europeans born in the Indies lose the courage of the European climate'[4]. All this not only meant that people would be poorer in warmer climates, it also meant that they were more likely to accept dictatorships, for 'servitude

4 Montesquieu, *The Spirit of the Laws*, p. 234.

always begins with drowsiness'[5]. Hence, democracies were more likely in colder places. A bit far-fetched, perhaps, but as the graph (Figure 3.2) shows, not completely barmy statistically, it is only the theory that seems a bit, well, fatalistic.

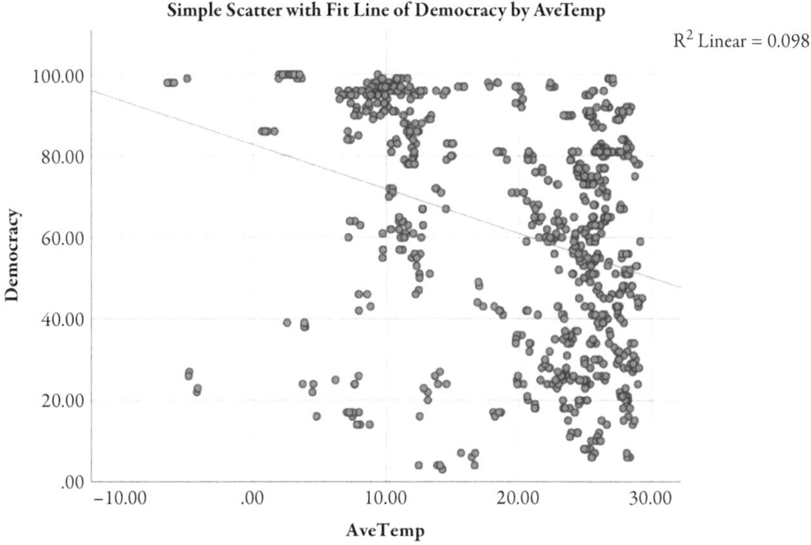

Figure 3.2 Democracy and Average Temperatures

For the gest of Montesquieu's argument was that there was little we could do; that prosperity was more or less proportional with geographic factors, and that the political system was a result of the same causes. It might be true. He might have been correct. It is a well-worn viewpoint. In fact, historically, it was quite common to believe that nations can do diddly squat if they were poor and unsuccessful, and underperform.

In ancient Greece, a view very similar to that of Montesquieu was common (the philosopher Aristotle also cited the climate as an important factor[6]), and our French nobleman was happy to concede that his theory

5 Montesquieu, *The Spirit of the Laws*, p. 243.

6 Aristotle (1944) *The Politics*. Cambridge MA: Harvard University Press, p. 567.

was anything but original. It seems a depressing conclusion. One we can do little about, although a distinguished professor at *Berkeley, University of California*, suggested that air conditioning, might mitigate the effects identified by Montesquieu[7].

Generally speaking, there has been no shortage of similar depressive theories. For example, the geographer Jared Mason Diamond's best-selling book *Guns, Germs, and Steel* won the *Pulitzer Prize* for arguing that its high diversity of wild plant and animal species suitable for domestication in Northern Europe, that gave the people there a head start. As a result of this, the northerners were able to subdue other cultures and peoples because they had an edge in the stone age[8]. In fact, there has been no end of fanciful theories of when countries, states and even cities are successful. An American academic recently suggested that cities had higher crime rates if people were 'bowling alone', rather than in organised leagues[9]. In short, if people would only follow the lead of the misfits of the movie *The Big Lebowski*, and live by the rule, 'fuck it lets go bowling', all the worlds' problems would be solved. It's just that compulsory ten-pin bowling is an unlikely candidate for a serious public policy. If everything depends on the weather, or the animals that roamed around us in the Neolithic, we might as well settle down with a drink, resign to fate and just 'cultivate our garden' – as Voltaire once said[10]. Whether this is so, is a question we shall return to. But first we need to survey the ley of the land. No structural engineer would start building before she knows the terrain and without knowing the laws of nature. Politics is the art not merely of knowing what we want but also of knowing what exists and understanding what is possible given the natural limits of our knowledge.

Still, we start with a bit of a disadvantage. Without sounding a too depressive note, sociologists have often been very good at identifying

7 Nelson W. Polsby (2004) *How Congress Evolves: Social Bases of Institutional Change*. Oxford: Oxford University Press, p. 80.

8 Jared M. Diamond (1998) *Guns, Germs and Steel: A Short History of Everybody for the Last 13,000 Years*. New York: Random House.

9 Putnam, Robert D. (1995) 'Bowling Alone: America's Declining Social Capital'. *Journal of Democracy* (6), 65–78.

10 François-Marie Voltaire (1993) *Candide*. New York: Dover, p. 167.

underlying patterns that we could do rather little about, at least in the short run. Maybe they are correct, maybe the world is a cruel and unfair place, where some draw the shortest straw in the game of life, and where others, whether deserving or not, get rich; the 'gods favour the strong', and the 'strong do what they can and the weak suffer what they must', as an ancient historian nonchalantly observed[11].

Many of the correlations proposed by sociologists and other writers have revolved around religion. Something we can do very little about. Our friend Montesquieu was not just fatalistic about the weather. He also believed that religion played a role. Though he was himself a Catholic, he was of the opinion that Protestants were more self-assured and confident as they were answerable directly to the Almighty. Conversely, the ones who could only communicate indirectly with the Lord, through intermediaries such as the Virgin Mary, the Saints and the Pope, would be less entrepreneurial. That a religion – something we cannot change immediately – could be the cause of greatness, or the opposite, is a well-worn theme among scholars. The eminent German sociologist Max Weber (who wrote his most celebrated books in the first two decades of the twentieth century) likewise argued that countries were more likely to be prosperous if the majority of the population were Protestants. The famous relationship between the legendary 'protestant ethics' and 'the spirit of capitalism' was, it must be admitted, not a simple one. It was *not* that protestants just worked harder. It was rather that they, in a complicated way, were looking for signs that they were among the chosen few, who, according to the Calvinist version of Protestantism, would be saved by the Lord on the Day of Judgement[12]. Whether this theory was at all plausible, whether Calvinists thought in this way at all is perhaps debatable. But the idea that Protestants were more successful than Catholics, made it legitimate to look at religion as a cause of prosperity.

In this day and age, even Calvinists and Catholics – unless they are especially keen – are unlikely to be able to distinguish the finer points of

11 Thucydides (1913). *The History of the Peloponnesian War*. London: J. M. Dent and Sons, p. 394.

12 Max Weber (2002). *The Protestant Ethic and the 'spirit' of Capitalism and Other Writings*. London: Penguin.

difference between their respective theological doctrines. The fundamental difference in modern societies is not between different sects or denominations of Christianity. But, in an increasingly multicultural world, the difference is between different religions; between Christians and Muslims, for example, and between those who believe in one or more deities, and those who, with different degrees of enthusiasm, vehemently, do not.

Gott mit Uns – 'God with Us', read an embroidery demonstratively placed over the door in my grandparents' house. They were devout, pious and economically conservative. Hard work was encouraged, often with a quote from Scripture. St Paul was a particular favourite; 'of the Lord ye shall receive the reward' was a common response to anything to do with work[13]. Jesus was rarely cited. Perhaps, the itinerant preacher, who described himself as 'a glutton and a drunkard, a friend of tax collectors and sinners', didn't quite fit the mould of pious protestant Evangelicals[14].

So, does a large number of devout Christians lead to more prosperity? In terms of statistics, the answer is negative. There is no correlation between the BPI-score and the proportion of Christians, nor is there any statistical association between the percentage of nominal followers of Jesus Christ and economic performance.

Equality is another central tenant in the Christian Bible. 'Blessed are the poor,' said Jesus, and St Paul spelled this out even more clearly, in words that appeared almost socialist: 'At the present time your plenty will supply what they need, so that in turn their plenty will supply what you need. The goal is equality.'[15] In this, the followers have not practised what they preach; there is a correlation between inequality and the proportion of Christians of 24 percent. More Christians equals a slightly higher level of inequality. Admittedly, this is not a massive association but certainly one that runs counter to the official teaching. None of the other world religions are statistically associated with inequality. The reasons for this might be hard to depict. Perhaps, it is the focus on hard work, that means that countries with a high proportion of Christians become more selfish, but this is difficult to measure statistically.

But it is not all doom and gloom. In the Sermon on the Mount, Jesus famously said, 'If anyone slaps you on the right cheek, turn to them the

13 Colossians 3: 23.

14 The Gospel according to St. Luke 7:34.

15 2 Corinthians 8.14.

other cheek also.'[16] Whether motivated by this spirit or not there is a negative correlation between Christians and the homicide of just -30 percent; more believers in Jesus means (statistically) fewer murders. An increase of one percent in the number of Christians will all other things being equal lower the homicide rate by one percent.

But Weber did not only write about Protestantism. He also wrote, about the religions originating in the South Asian continent, such as Buddhism. By contrast to Islam, he was surprised to find that salvation (getting to *Nirvana*) was possible to 'only a few, even of those who have resolved to live in poverty, chastity and unemployment'. The Buddhist tradition was characterised by 'other-worldliness', and for this reason, 'there evolved no capitalist spirit'. Keen not to appear preachy – Weber was an exceptionally open-minded man for his time – he found 'no proof whatever that a weaker natural endowment for technical economic rationalism was responsible for the actual difference in this respect'[17].

But that was a long time ago. Have things stayed the same or have they changed? Focussing on economics, as Weber did (albeit he did this without access to statistical tools and *Big Data*), we find a strong negative correlation of -62 between Buddhism and economic output per Capita, as is well-illustrated by the graph (Figure 3.3).

But why exactly have Buddhist countries been so relatively unsuccessful? One explanation is that many people give money to monasteries. A study has shown that in Thailand, the proportion given to monks was as high as '55% of the total income'. For a rational individual, who wants to go to Nirvana, this makes sense, if the deeds are rewarded by better *Karma*. However, in terms of economic growth, it is less likely to be a fruitful strategy, as 'the more that the laity give to monks … the less the economy grows'. But, of course, there are other important things in life than a high GDP[18]. Reaching Nirvana is, for a devout person, infinitely more important than the bank balance in this life.

16 The Gospel According to St Matthew, 5.39.

17 Max Weber (2013) *Economy and Society*. Berkeley, CA: University of California Press, pp. 628–630.

18 All quotes from S. Zadek (1993) 'The Practice of Buddhist Economics? Another View'. *American Journal of Economics and Sociology*, 52(4), 433–445.

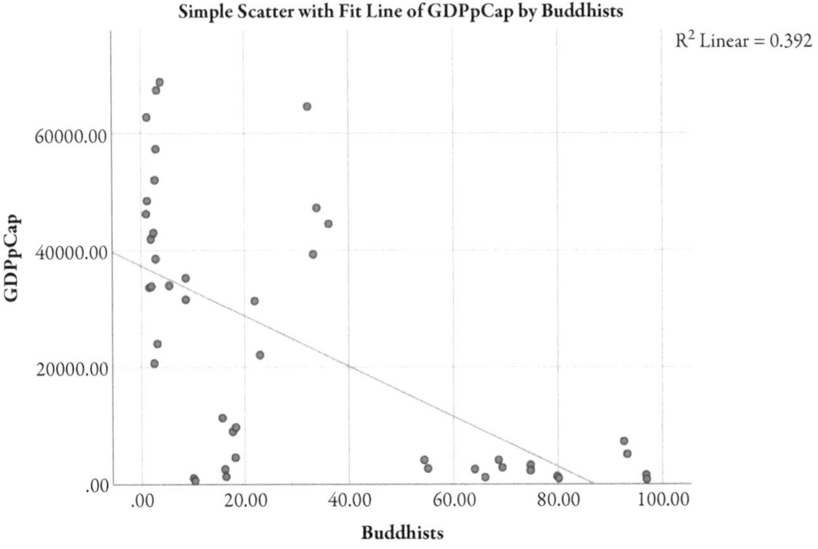

Figure 3.3 Proportion of Buddhists and GDP per Capita

In this book we are interested in more than just cool cash. But while the negative correlation is not quite as massive between BPI and the proportion of Buddhists in a country, it is still considerable at just under -40 percent. In other words, more Buddhists are associated with a lower score on the Better Place Index. This might be due to historical reasons. The predominately Buddhist countries (like, for example, Thailand, Sri Lanka and Myanmar) were exploited by imperialist Western countries and we set back in their developments. The relationships between religion and social and economic outcomes are not simple and the results of single causes. Still, the correlations tell a story that cannot be ignored.

However, while Buddhism may not be able to generate much economic growth, it is associated with more peaceful societies. Peace comes from within. Do not seek it without', said Siddhārtha (later known as the Buddha). And, those who have followed in his footsteps *have* been rather peaceful; there is a negative correlation of -40 between Buddhists and the murder rate, more Buddhists fewer homicides.

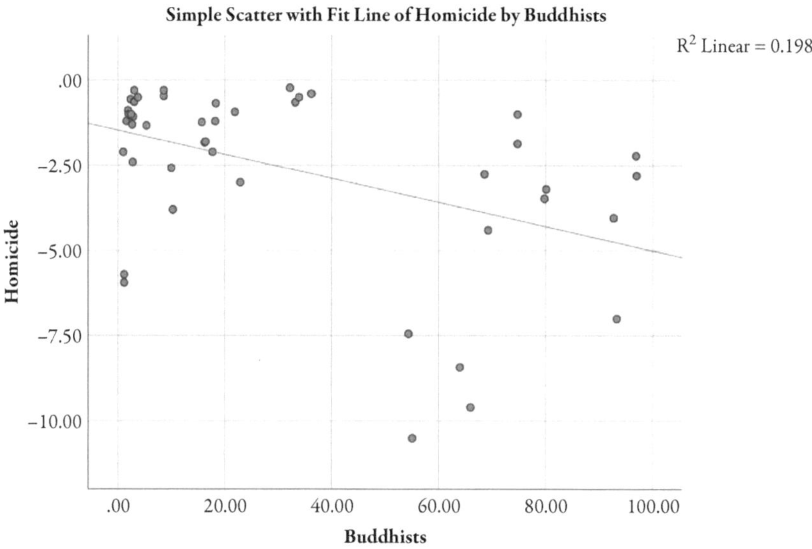

Figure 3.4 Homicide Rates and Proportion of Buddhists

This is certainly reassuring for Buddhists. But the problem is that countries where there are many adherents to this belief-system generally score rather lowly on the other indicators that make up the Better Place Index. This is perhaps surprising. 'For thousands of years,' wrote a Buddhist monk,

> the Buddhist forest monasteries have manifested a harmonious living with nature … Tranquil life in the forest helped Buddhist practitioners to improve their inner mind … The harmonious living of Buddhism is completely different from the competitive … living and fighting against the nature as seen in the West … which tends to destruction for selfish gains[19].

In reality, environmental protection is anything but associated with this belief-system. The correlation between the proportion of Buddhists and CO2 emissions is a whopping 65 percent. The only other religion

19 *Thich Tri Quang, Buddhism and Environmental Protection*, <https://www.budsas.org/ebud/ebdha006.htm>. Accessed 24 June 2020.

to be associated with environmental degradation is the Christians, albeit at a much lower level (just above 20 percent). It would appear that the Buddhists have been a bit too focused on what the monk called 'their inner mind', to pay full attention to the pollution of the nature around them.

Hinduism, the other great religion of South Asia, is known – perhaps in slight caricature – for the caste system; for *Rta* – the divine cosmic order, and for the stipulation that, 'all men keep their proper place and discharge their proper *Dharma*'[20]. One would perhaps have expected that a religion with this belief-system would associated with vast inequalities.

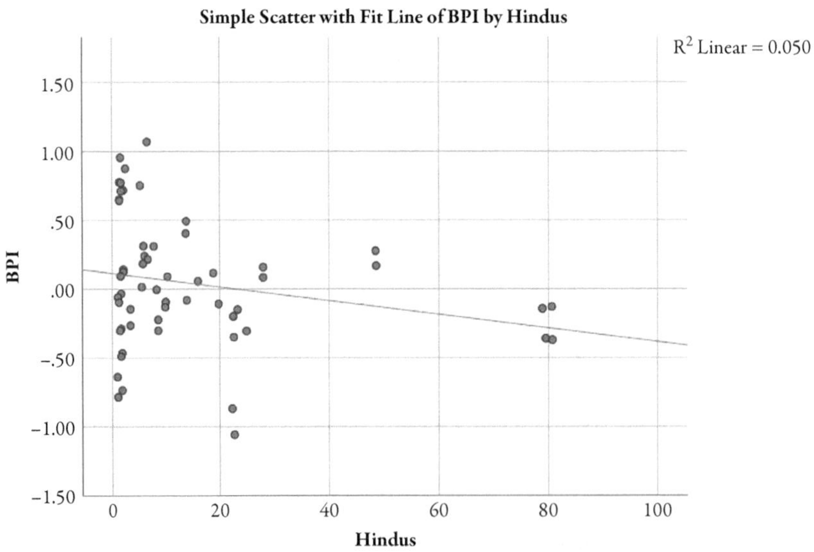

Figure 3.5 Proportion of Hindus and BPI

Yet this is not the case. There is no correlation between the proportion of Hindus in a country and economic inequality.

But in other ways, societies with a large proportion of adherents of this religion are not so fortunate in other respects. The correlation between

20 Bhinku C. Parakh (1991) 'Hindu Political Thought', in David Miller et al. (Editors) *The Blackwell Encyclopaedia of Political Thought*. Oxford: Blackwell, pp. 205–206.

the percentage of Hindus and GDP per Capita is a negative -33, and there is a slight negative correlation between the proportion of Hindus and the score on the Better Place Index, though not a massive one at -22.

There might be any number of reasons for this relationship, and the issue is certainly more complex than what can be accounted for in a few paragraphs. But the less than impressive correlations would not surprise observers, even ones who adhere to this tradition. Raj Krishna, a distinguished Indian economist, has even coined the term 'the Hindu Growth Rate', to contrast it to other, more successful, Asian economies[21]. Of course, it might be argued, that India has caught up, and that this particular Hindu dominated country has made strides since then. But, as we saw in Chapter 1, the positive tendencies have been somewhat reversed in the past few years. Could there be an underlying reason for the negative statistical relationship more generally between the proportion of Hindus and the poor performance on the Better Place Index? Could tradition be part of it? It does not seem too far-fetched to suggest that the rigid caste system impedes entrepreneurship. In fact, the evidence supports this, and it has recently been proven that 'low- and middle-caste individuals … lack access to modern capital markets,' and that 'the historically disadvantaged castes are less likely to enter entrepreneur-ship' as a result of this[22]. But this only accounts for the financial side of things. It doesn't explain the short life expectancy, and the less than impressive scores on our education measure, except that all of these are associated with economic output. There is a strong correlation between GDP per Capita and life expectancy of just over 60, so being poor impacts other factors.

The Hindu tradition has been rich on good governance. Kautilya – the second BCE political thinker famous for the saying 'your enemy's enemy is your friend' – wrote what he called *Arthasastra*. Politics, as he defined it was '[the], art of 'maintaining territory and promoting its prosperity'[23]. But much as Hindu writers have pondered this, countries dominated by

21 K. Sen (2009). 'What a Long, Strange Trip It's been: Reflections on the Causes of India's Growth Miracle'. *Contemporary South Asia*, 17 (4), 363–377.

22 S. S. Goraya (2019). 'How does Caste Affect Entrepreneurship? Birth vs Worth, Barcelona GSE Paper Series, Working Paper n° 1104, p. 38

23 Kautilya quoted in Parakh, 'Hindu Political Thought', p. 205.

this religion have not been successful in converting the good intentions into a better society overall. But, then again, nor have many other religions. These findings might be controversial in India, but they are unlikely to even divide opinion there. Is it different with Islam?

Many politicians, especially those on the far-right, are likely to find every possible flaw with anything associated with Islam, whereas those on the other side of politics are likely to downplay any negative effects associated with this religion. We are not concerned with petty political argument based on pure prejudice and lazy assumptions. While facts can be biased, asking questions about prosperity and scores on the Better Place Index is relatively free of prejudice. So, what does the data tell us?

The relationship between the percentage of Muslims in a society and the score on the Better Place Index is, according to the data, negative. But not by much. The correlation between BPI and the proportion of adherents to Islam is -28, but as the graph (Figure 3.6) shows, there are several outliers. Thus, there are successful countries with a large proportion of Muslims, for example, Singapore (with roughly fifteen percent).

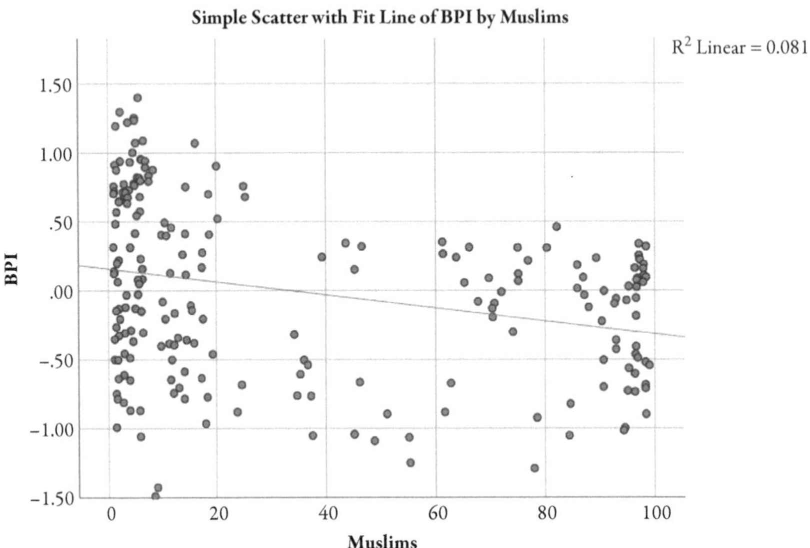

Figure 3.6 Proportion of Muslims and BPI

It is useful to look at some of the individual factors. For example, some Muslim countries are very rich (to name but a few, Qatar, Saudi Arabia and Kuwait). So, is there a correlation between this variable and the proportion of people who profess Islam as their religion?

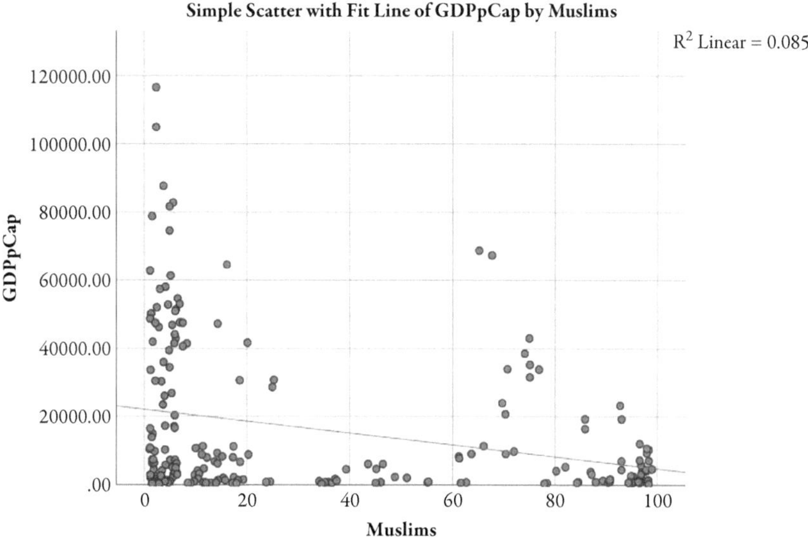

Figure 3.7 GDP per Capita and the Proportion of Muslims

Yes, but a negative one. The statistical relationship between the proportion of Muslims in a society and the economic output as measured by GDP per Capita is -30. Though with a score like this there are outliers, as we can see from the graph (Figure 3.7). But overall, a large proportion of devout Muslims is inversely correlated with the Index, and with economic output.

Why is this so? To answer this is not simple or easy. Any conclusions regarding the effects of religious belief systems and social and economic outcomes must come with a scholarly health warning and are bound to be controversial. And this is especially true of Islam. Regarding Muslim societies, it has been rightly said that

> the world's Muslim-majority countries are spread across three continents, and substantial Muslim minorities exist in other parts of the world. Surely the practice of

> Islam varies geographically, depending on local circumstances and influences .... But exceptions alone do not invalidate a generalization. In scholarship, as opposed to polemical literatures ... a generalization's validity depends on the existence of an identifiable social mechanism that explains a common pattern[24].

One of these 'generalisations' could be the evidence that economic productivity goes down during *Ramadan*. However, all is not economics. The same research suggested that those who observed ritual fasting tended to be happier and have a more positive outlook on life[25]. Certainly, not all figures suggest that Islam is negatively correlated with the measures that comprise the Better Place Index. For example, there is no statistical association between homicide and the proportion of Muslims, nor between this religion or life expectancy. But education is certainly shorter in Muslim countries (a negative correlation of -31 percent), something that has been attributed to fewer educational opportunities for women in countries with a large proportion of Muslims[26]. So, overall, and when we add up the scores, countries with a large proportion of adherents to Islam do badly on the Better Place Index.

This, once again, could be explained by historical factors, and be a result of a phenomenon known among scholars as *Path Dependency*. Basically, that embedded and deep cultural traditions create circumstances that it is difficult to overcome. The ban on interests or *Riba* – which previously also existed in Christian cultures (where it was called 'Usury') – has meant that banks in largely Islamic countries do not have the same access to finance to fund projects as do their counterparts in other parts of the world, especially in the West. As a result of this, studies have shown that 'long-term financing is rarely offered to entrepreneurs'[27]. Cultural factors, to put it differently, mean that those in countries with many Muslims have tended to lose out

24 Timur Kuran (2018) 'Islam and Economic Performance: Historical and Contemporary Links'. *Journal of Economic Literature*, 56(4), 1292–1359.

25 Filipe Campante, and David Yanagizawa-Drott (2015) 'Does Religion Affect Economic Growth and Happiness? Evidence from Ramadan.' *Quarterly Journal of Economics,* 130(2), 615–658.

26 David S. Landes, and Richard A. Landes (2001) Girl Power: Do Fundamentalists Fear Our Women? New Republic. October 8: 20–23.

27 Rajesh K. Aggarwal and Tarik Yousef (2000) 'Islamic Banks and Investment Financing.' *Journal of money, credit and banking,* 32(1), 93–120, at p. 93.

more or less directly as a result of a cultural norm or rather the religious command that 'for their taking Riba they were prohibited'[28]. There were good reasons for introducing this ban in the seventh century CE. Before Islam, many were enslaved because they could not pay their debts because of excessive interests. Certainly, excessive interest rates can lead to hardship. But the flipside of a total ban is that finance is less likely to be available. In addition to this, the 'Classical Islamic law recognizes only natural persons; it does not grant standing to corporations', and it becomes clearer why a large proportion of Muslims are inversely correlated with capitalist development and entrepreneurship[29]. Simply, the factors that facilitated economic growth were not there and were actively discouraged, if not outright banned. And, as most other factors on the Better Place Index are correlated with good economic outcomes, this cultural factor has an impact on the BPI-score.

So, none of the big world religions are unequivocally associated with positives. Yes, countries with many Buddhists and with many Christians have lower homicide rates, but apart from this, across the board, a large number of religious followers are associated with lower BPI-scores.

So, suppose we take the opposite position, and we look at the relationship between those who do *not* adhere to a religion and the scores on the Index. Does that make a difference how godly a country is? It seems to be the case that more agnostics are good for the economy.

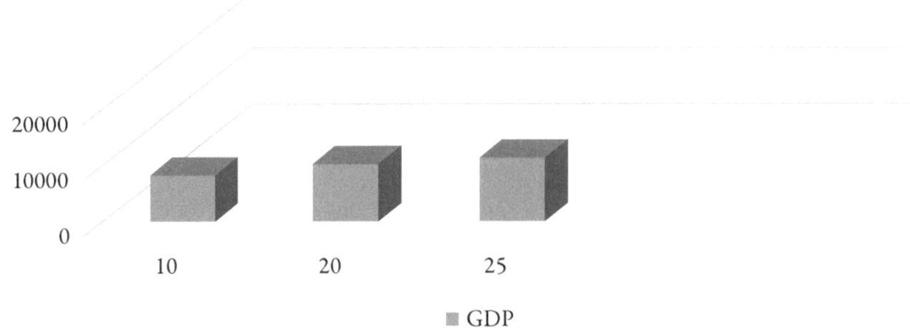

Figure 3.8 Proportion of Agnostics and GDP per Capita

28 Quran, 4.161.

29 Timur Kuran (2005) 'The Absence of the Corporation in Islamic Law: Origins and Persistence'. *The American Journal of Comparative Law*, *53*(4), 785–834.

At least the GDP per Capita slightly rises the more religiously unaffiliated citizens there are. The correlation between economic output and the proportion of agnostics (here measured by those unaffiliated with any particular religion) is positive – at just over thirty-four. It was either neutral or negative where there were many believers. Further, we find a slightly higher correlation of forty when we correlated the proportion of nonbelievers with the Better Place Index.

Moreover, a high proportion of agnostics is correlated with longer education (a correlation of just over forty), a longer life (a correlation of thirty-five), and the more godless countries pollute less (at -25, there is a negative correlation between CO_2 emissions and the proportion of unbelievers).

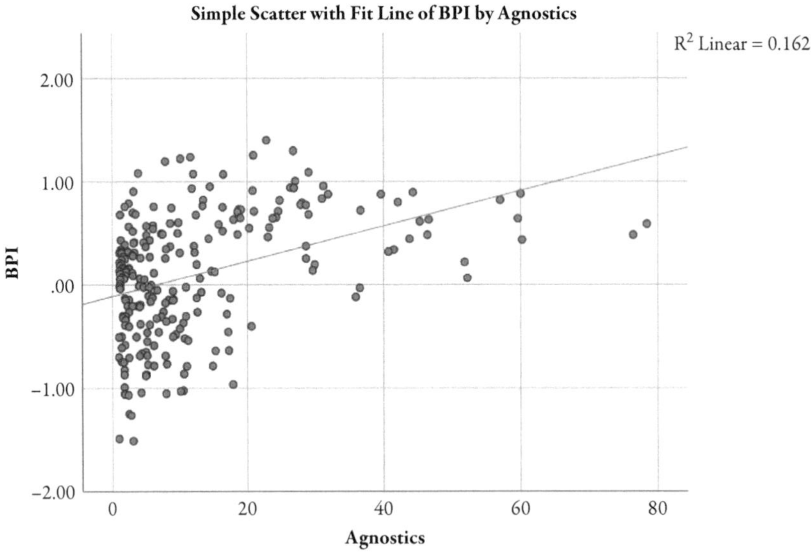

Figure 3.9 BPI and the Proportion of Agnostics

Again, these correlations could be due to all sorts of other factors and they do not constitute facts. For example, it could be that unbelievers tend to live in colder places (there is a negative correlation between the average temperature and the proportion of agnostics of -46 – colder climates are associated with less organised religious observance). It could also be, and these different explanations may be complementary, that those who are not religious are more likely to focus on the life on earth here and now, whereas professed believers are more concerned with the afterlife, their future rebirth, or progressing towards Nirvana, and thus have a different and literally 'otherworldly' focus.

All this is not, of course, to say that religion is not important for the good life, or even to question the veracity of any of the religions in what we might call any metaphysical sense. Statistics and social science theories – or any theories for that matter – cannot prove (or otherwise) matters of religious faith. But the findings suggest, perhaps, that a too close focus on religion is detrimental to achieving the goals associated with good government. Religion and politics rarely mix, or so the evidence suggests. Perhaps Jesus Christ himself felt the same when he said that 'my kingdom is not of this world'[30], and that we should 'render unto Caesar the things that are Caesar's, and unto God the things that are God's'[31].

But all these matters, interesting though the correlations might be, belong to the world of despondent defeatism; to things we can do precious little about. These findings are depressing for policy makers as they do not provide a quick and easy fix – or even a long-term one.

To be sure, we could ban religion – as they tried in Albania under the particularly harsh version of Communism under Enver Hoxha. That, to put it mildly, did not improve well-being. The GDP per Capita in the last decade of the life of the small Communist state was US$750. In Greece, that had just come out of a decade of an autocratic right-wing dictatorship, by contrast, had a value of economic output per person that was just under $5,000 per year.

Are there other factors? Some philosophers have suggested that smaller places are more successful. Plato, through his mouthpiece *The Athenian*, recommended that a state should have no more than 5,040 citizens – which with slaves, women and children would be about ten times as many inhabitants[32]. This would make the best possible state a little bit larger, in terms of population, than Liechtenstein with 37,000 people and slightly smaller than St Kitts and Nevis at 60,000.

30 St John, 18:36.

31 Matt: 22.21.

32 Plato, *The Laws*, Book V.

So, it was a popular theory in the minds of illustrious men that it was good to be a small state – at least as far as a good life was concerned. 'Practically all small states, whether they are republics or monarchies prosper merely by reason of the fact that they are small,' wrote the famous philosopher Jean-Jacques Rousseau when he was asked, as a kind of management consultant, to come up with suggestions for a new system of government for Poland back in 1770[33]. But, of course, *le philosophe*, wrote before we had statistical analysis. And, contrary to what Rousseau thought, there is absolutely no correlation whatsoever between size and success. The much-cited claim that 'small is beautiful' – that was made famous by a book with the same name, was much in vogue among certain romantics in a bygone age, and still has its adherents[34].

It's just that the facts don't stack up statistically. Yes, some of the countries that score highly on the Better Place Index are small, Luxembourg, for example. But others are big, Germany to name but one. And, we cannot cherry-pick cases without prior justification. That is the attraction of statistics. Overall, size does not matter for a nation. The correlation between BPI and population size is equally non-existent at -0.5 percent. Just as well, it would be difficult, as a deliberate policy to forcibly break up states.

Women in Power

A man once said that 'nations stumble upon establishments, which are indeed the result of human action but not the execution of any human design'[35], and he went on to say that policies originate 'from the instincts,

33 Jean-Jacques Rousseau (1986) 'Considerations on the Government of Poland', in Frederick Watkins (Editor) *Jean-Jacques Rousseau: Political Writings*. Madison, WI: The University of Wisconsin Press, p. 181.

34 Ernst Friedrich Schumacher (2011) *Small Is Beautiful: A Study of Economics as If People Mattered*. Random House.

35 Adam Fergusson (1996) *An Essay on the History of Civil Society*. Cambridge: Cambridge University Press, p. 187.

not the speculations of men'[36]. The gendered language is clearly out of date, and perhaps even literally so. For example, it is conceivable that developments might be a result of 'speculations' and 'human action' by women.

Measuring gender inequality – equality between the sexes is everywhere a long way off – is a tricky issue. In this we shall rely on the proportion of female members of parliament. Not, because it is the best measure of female influence, but because it is one of the few reliable measures we have.

So, does it make a difference if women are in a position of power and influence? A simple way of gauging this is to see if more female MPs are associated with better outcomes on the Better Place Index and a higher GDP per Capita. The statistical data suggest that there is a correlation. For example, countries with more than 25 percent women members of parliament have an average BPI of 0.13. The countries that have less than this proportion have a minus score on the Better Place Index of, on average -0.05.

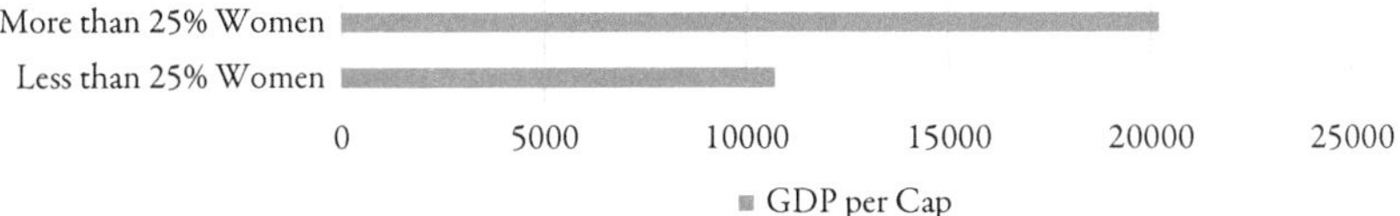

Figure 3.10 GDP per Capita and Women MPs

The same positive tendencies of having a higher proportion of female parliamentarians can be seen in the countries' economic performance. As Figure 3.10 shows, at $20,190 the countries with more than 25 percent females in parliaments have a GDP per Capita that is almost twice that of countries that fall below this threshold (the ones with fewer women in the national legislature only have an average GDP per person of $10,707). Statistically speaking for every 1 percent increase in the proportion of female MPs, the average citizen makes another $382 per year.

A more scientific approach is to determine if there is a correlation between the proportion of female MPs and the Better Place Index. As the graph Figure 3.11 shows, there is a statistical link between more women

36 Ibid.

members of parliament and a higher score on the Better Place Index, though in terms of raw numbers the correlation is only twenty-four.

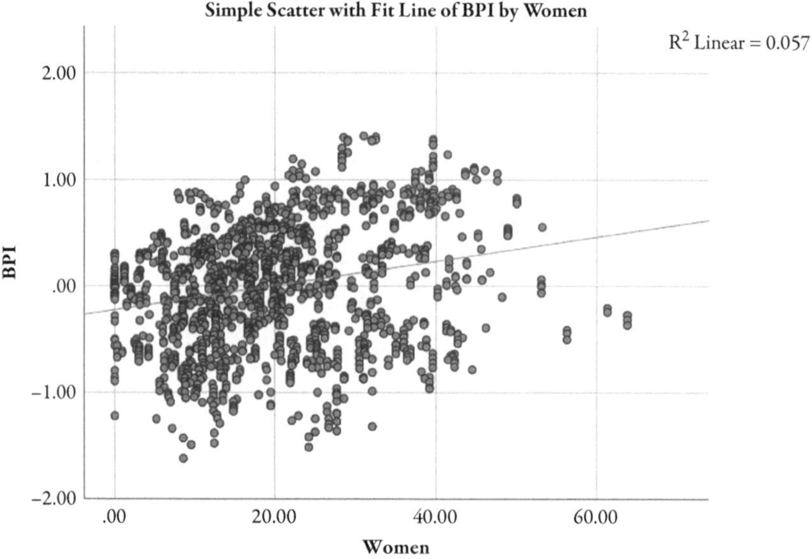

Figure 3.11 BPI and Percentage of Female MPs

The same relationship is found when we correlate the proportion of female legislators with GDP per Capita. Here the correlation is slightly higher, namely thirty-four.

These positive tendencies are accompanied by other trends, such as a correlation between spending on health care there is a positive association between the amount of public spending allocated to health and the proportion of women MPs of thirty percent, and between women legislators and the number of doctors per 100,000 inhabitants of just under twenty-six percent. On put in perhaps more understandable terms, for every three percent increase in the number of female MPs we get another doctor per 10,000 people.

But, again, these are merely numbers, and statistical figures do not by themselves constitute facts unless they are backed up by explanations. So, what accounts for the mostly positive effects of having more women legislators? This question has surprisingly received scarce attention by statisticians.

In the main those writing about the positive effects of more female involvement in legislation have been based on small case studies, and more often than not, interviews and micro-research that may not be representative.

For example, in a very influential book the psychologist Carol Gilligan, suggested that, unlike men 'the development of women's moral judgement appears to proceed from an initial concern with survival to focus on goodness and principled understanding of non-violence'[37]. The positive effects of more doctors and more spending on health would seem to support this so-called *ethics of care* argument.

This sociological theory has been supported by more case studies especially in the legal system. For example, female judges focus more on the ethics of care and compassion[38]. And in 'employment discrimination cases, female judges were significantly more liberal than their male colleagues'[39]. The reason for this, it has been speculated, is that when the number of women reached a certain threshold, policies would begin to be gentler and more focused on 'softer values'[40]. Yet, the interesting thing here is that more women MPs, senators, representatives and so on, does *not* correlate with better education, lower infant mortality, longer life or better environmental protection, that is with the policy goals that are associated with the feminist ethics of care.

The percentage of female parliamentarians is simple not correlated with any of these factors. And nor is there any tendency that more MPs result in more equality. More women MPs – which up to a point indicated

37 Carol Gilligan (1977) 'In a Different Voice: Women's Conceptions of Self and of Morality'. *Harvard Educational Review*, 47(4), 481–517, at p. 515.

38 S. Davis (1992) 'Do Women Judges Speak in a Different Voice--Carol Gilligan, Feminist Legal Theory, and the Ninth Circuit.' *Wis. Women's Law Journal*, 8, 143.

39 Donald R. Songer, Sue Davis, and Susan Haire (May 1994) 'A Reappraisal of Diversification in the Federal Courts: Gender Effects in the Courts of Appeals'. *The Journal of Politics*, 56(2), 425–439.

40 D. Dahlerup, R. Campbell, and S. Childs (2014). *The Critical Mass Theory in Public and Scholarly Debates*. Colchester: ECPR Press, p. 137.

greater equality between the sexes – is not universally associated with a perfect society, though there is a tendency that that a higher female representation in politics is associated with a better health system – as expected by feminists – and better economic outcomes. Maybe, Margaret Thatcher had a point when she told the Conservative Party conference in 1979 that the economy was in safe hands with a 'housewife with a weekly budget to balance'.

Migration

Another factor that is often debated – perhaps even more harshly and uncompromisingly than religion and gender – is immigration. Some of the celebrated classical philosophers, were none too keen on immigration. One philosopher who is often held in high regard among so-called *progressives on the left*, wanted to ban foreigners from teaching[41].

Movement of people across borders has not become less controversial over time. It is also often unpopular. For example, no less than '63 percent of French people believe that too many immigrants are living in their country'[42]. Contemporary researchers writing about this have speculated that the effect of it might be negative. Thus, if the newcomers 'lack the skills that employers demand and find it difficult to adapt, immigration may significantly increase the costs associated with income maintenance programs as well as exacerbate the ethnic wage differentials already in existence in the host country'[43]. Until the 1990s, migrants were 'more likely to receive welfare assistance than earlier immigrants, and also more likely to do so than natives: 21 percent of immigrant households participate[d] in some means-tested social-assistance program (such as cash benefits,

41 Jean-Jacques Rousseau (1986) 'Considerations on the Government of Poland', in Frederick Watkins (Editor) *Jean-Jacques Rousseau: Political Writings*. Madison: University of Wisconsin Press, pp. 159–274, at. p. 177.

42 David Frum (2019) 'How Much Immigration is Too Much?'. *The Atlantic*, 323(3), 64–74, at 66.

43 George J Borjas, 'The Economics of Immigration'. *Journal of Economic Literature*. 32(4), 1667–1717, p. 1667.

Medicaid, or food stamps), as compared with 14 percent of native households'[44]. This, however, changed after the Welfare Reforms enacted under President Clinton in the late 1990s. As of the most recent figures, the situation has reversed: 'On average, each immigrant who is broadly eligible for the welfare or entitlement programs costs $16,088 in 2016, about 27 percent less than the average native who costs $21,926.'[45] This might explain why some of a more free-market and small-government persuasion have tended to take the view, that migration is good for the economy, as migrants, in the jargon, just supply a demand. The *Cato Institute*, a free-market or libertarian thinktank, economically on the Republican right, even claimed that 'immigrant entrepreneurship is an important driver of innovation and firm creation in the United States'. Once again statistics, while never the last word on any subject, provides an answer.

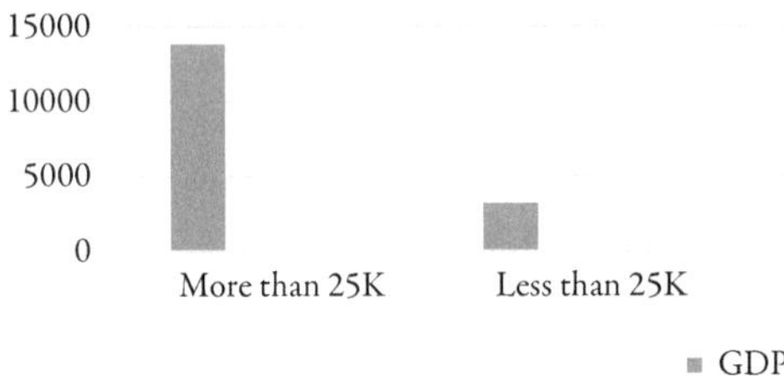

Figure 3.12 GDP per Capita and Number of Migrants per 100,000

As the Figure 3.12 shows, countries that have more than 25,000 migrants per 100,000 inhabitants have a GDP per Capita that is over $10,000 higher than states that have fewer than this number. The countries with more migrants, on average, have a GDP per Capita of $13,836. Those with lower numbers, by contrast produce goods and services to the value of a mere $3,209 per year.

44 George J. Borjas (1996) 'The New Economics of Immigration'. *The Atlantic Monthly*, 278(5), 72–80, at p. 76.

45 Alex Nowrasteh and Robert Orr (2018) 'Immigration and the Welfare State: Immigrant and Native Use Rates and Benefit Levels for Means-Tested Welfare and Entitlement Programs', *The Cato Institute, Immigration Research and Policy Brief No. 6*

Of course, such figures can be arbitrary, and to do our analysis properly we cannot simply rely on averages and percentages. We need to look at more general tendencies, and for this, correlations are, again, the most useful tool.

So, what does the statistics tell us? They are almost as conclusive as they can be in the social sciences. There is a 58 percent correlation between economic growth and the proportion of migrants per 100,000 inhabitants. Statistically this is exceptionally high, and the sort of correlation that is very rare in the social sciences. In the debate about immigration, and its effects on society as a whole, the positions are often polarised, and they are rarely based on a dispassionate analysis. But if we were to look at the matter without prejudice, we would find that more immigration is significantly correlated with longer life expectancy (37 percent), with more education (the correlation is 32 percent), and with more hospital beds (25 percent).

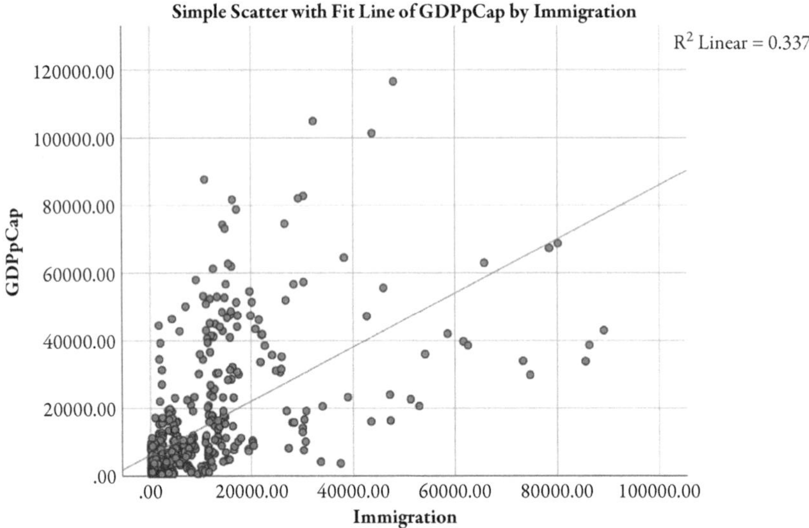

Figure 3.13 GDP per Capita and Immigration

That many migrants – especially those from South Asia – often achieve better exam results translates into more doctors. For example, while the proportion of South Asians (Indians, Bangladeshi and Pakistanis) in the

United Kingdom stands at just under 3 percent, the proportion of medical doctors of this ethnic group constitute 27 percent of all members of the *British Medical Association*[46].

These almost universally positive tendencies associated with people moving to a country translate into a correlation between immigration and the Better Place Index of a very respectable 33 percent. Thus, the positive statistical data regarding immigration are much stronger than those associated with any of the correlations between religions we discussed earlier in this chapter and also stronger than the statistical effects of having more female MPs. In terms of statistical association, especially the correlation between migrants and economic output is nothing less than astounding. Yet, as always, there are caveats. Some will question if the positive effects are shared equally across society and, indeed, if the migrants themselves benefit. These questions cannot be answered by looking at the datasets for the B*etter Place Index* and requires us to look elsewhere.

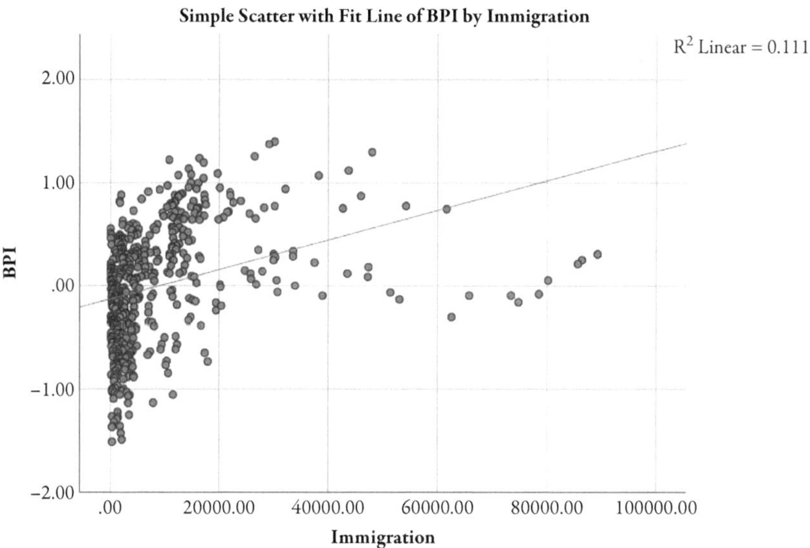

Figure 3.14. BPI and Immigration

46 Isobel Bowler (2004) 'Ethnic Profile of the Doctors in the United Kingdom'. *British Medical Journal*, 329.583–584.

There are some indications that the newcomers themselves fare poorly. For example, in America, 'the fact remains that the wage of Mexican-American natives is itself 16 percent below that of the typical U.S [citizen]'[47]. There is also a perception, among some, that certain income groups are detrimentally affected by immigration, in a pithy – though not necessarily correct – summary of one commentator: 'Affluent Americans gain; poor Americans lose.'[48] This is not backed up by statistics but the view – erroneous or not – is widespread, and perhaps explains the political potency of the anti-immigrant rhetoric of certain political groups and parties. But the smaller relative gains for working class voters vis-à-vis their middle-class compatriots do not detract from the net overall economic yield. The Italian sociologist Vilfredo Pareto, who lived at the beginning of the twentieth century, considered a policy to be optimal if some people were better off, and nobody worse off[49]. Thus, migration is an example of what social scientists call a *Pareto Optimal* situation. The evidence, as the figures based on our data show, almost all point to the positive benefits of migration, and confirm the economic case for welcoming more people. The conclusion reached by a think tank in Washington seems apt and to the point:

> President Harry Truman famously quipped that he wanted a one-handed economist so they would actually reach agreement and form firm policy recommendations … [The] firm conclusions … [of] the academic literature … even a one-handed economist could firmly grasp: the economic benefits of immigration outweigh the costs[50].

However, the gains might be overlooked if some feel relative stagnation while others are much better off. This begs the question if immigration leads to more or less inequality? Senator Bernie Sanders, a one-time front-runner for the Democrat nomination for president, believed that more migrants would lead to lower wages, and hence more inequality, and be popular among the monied classes, Bring in all kinds of people,

47 Borjas, 'The economics of immigration', p. 1683.

48 Borjas, 'The new economics of immigration', p. *72*.

49 Vilfredo Pareto (2014) *Manual of Political Economy: A Critical and Variorum Edition*. OUP Oxford, p. 40.

50 A. Nowrasteh (2017) 'Introduction: The Economics of Immigration'. *Cato Journal*, 37(3), 445–447, at 447.

work of $2 or $3 an hour, that would be great for them [the rich]'[51]. As it happens, more immigration *does not* lead to more inequality. In fact, the opposite is true. As the graph (Figure 3.15) shows there is actually a negative relationship between immigration and inequality.

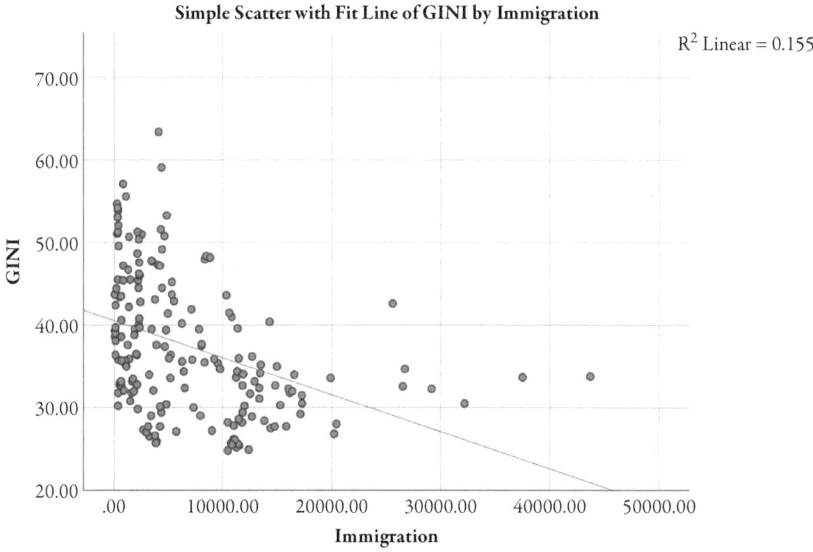

Figure 3.15 GINI Inequality and Immigration

The more people come to a country the more equal it becomes. In raw figures, the correlation is a negative -40, which is very respectable. Immigration means that everybody is better off. No one is stagnating. This is even more positive than Pareto could have dreamt of. Or, to put it differently, for every migrant that enters a country each individual gains an additional 0.79 US Dollars. That is, for every-one hundred migrants per 100,000 inhabitants, the average citizens gains just under $800. The effects of immigration are economically positive, and more migrants are conducive to creating a Better Place.

But the question is if migration, is like the weather or religion, something we cannot change, or something that is a given?

51 Senator Sanders quoted in Frum 'How Much Immigration is Too Much? p. 66.

As immigration is almost entirely a positive, we might wonder whether it is something that is subject to political influence, something that can be directly encouraged through deliberate public policies or by creating particular, so-called *Pull-Factors* that make a country more attractive for foreigners?

While we shall return to the effect of different kinds of political institutions in the next chapter, suffice it to say here that migrants are significantly *less* likely to travel to countries with presidential systems – there is a negative correlation of a whopping -54 – and are rather more likely to travel to countries with parliamentary systems like Sweden and the UK.

In the latter case there is a modest correlation of 23 percent. Migrants are also attracted to come to countries that score highly on measures of Due Process (a correlation of 45 percent) and the Rule of Law (a correlation of 43 percent).

Ethnic Groups

Up to a point most would accept at least some migration of people from other countries. The argument is not over either/or, but a matter of how many or how few. But there are also cultural factors that determine if a country can thrive, and even survive. More immigrants cannot be seen in isolation. Even if they adopt the lifestyle of their new country, there is likely to be trouble and discontent.

A sociological theory has suggested that countries are less likely to endure if they are split into different ethnic groups that lack a common narrative. If, so was the argument, there was merely a hotchpotch of different ethnic groups, there would be no common bond, and the country would fall apart if it didn't have a substantial majority that belonged to a dominant ethnic group or a *Staatsvolk*[52].

52 Brendan O'Leary (2001). 'An Iron Law of Nationalism and Federation?: A (Neo-Diceyian) Theory of the Necessity of a Federal Staatsvolk, and of Consociational Rescue'. *Nations and Nationalism*, 7(3), 273–296. It should be noted that this theory pertained only to federations but the principle would also apply to centralised states.

That societies can only really live peacefully and prosperously together if they are a homogeneous group, of course flies in the face of the liberal ideal of multiculturalism, that downplay these differences. Yet, even liberal politicians like former US President Barack Obama admitted, 'When I see Mexican flags waved at pro-immigration demonstrations, I feel a certain patriotic flus of patriotic resentment. When I am forced to use a translator to communicate with the guy who is fixing my car, I feel a certain frustration.'[53] But the case for a homogeneous society is an old one that was taken more or less for granted by even the classical philosophers of the liberal tradition. In the 1850s, the English MP and writer John Stuart Mill felt that running a government was 'next to impossible in a country made up of different nationalities'[54]. And across the Atlantic, half a century earlier, the men who drafted the U.S. Constitution in Philadelphia in 1787 were in no doubt that the establishment of the United States was only possible because the would-be citizens of the new federation constituted a people, with the same culture, the same language and the same creed. As one of them said at the time,

> providence has been pleased to give this one connected country to one united people – a people descended from the same ancestors, speaking the same language, professing the same religion, attached to the same principles of government, very similar in their manners and customs, and who, by their joint counsels, arms, and efforts, fighting side by side throughout a long and bloody war, have nobly established general liberty and independence[55].

But is there any justification for the view that countries must be homogenous to be successful, or even viable? Demographers and economists have developed a measure of how diverse countries are – it is known as the *Ethnic Fractionalisation Index* – in effect a statistical measure of multiculturalism[56]. Does this correlate with the Better Place Index? Or, is there a negative association as expected by contemporary social scientists and classic philosophers? As Figure 3.16 shows, there is indeed a negative

53 Barack Obama (2008) *The Audacity of Hope*. London: Canongate, p. 265.

54 John Stuart Mill, 'Considerations on Representative Government', p. 429.

55 Publius (1961) *Federalist Papers*. New York, Signet, p. 32.

56 Alberto Alesina, Arnaud Devleeschauwer, William Easterly, Sergio Kurlat, and Romain Wacziarg (2003) 'Fractionalization'. *Journal of Economic Growth,* 8(2), 155–194.

correlation between ethnic diversity and the Better Place Index. The statistical association ticks in at a very high -51 percent.

While there is no correlation of any kind between homicide and multi-ethnic states, let alone between the latter and CO_2 emissions, it is remarkable that countries with many ethnic groups have low life expectancy (a correlation of -52 percent) and that they tend to fare poorly on economic measures – though the correlation between GDP and multiculturalism is only -24.

Why is it that these countries with many ethnic groups score badly especially on health? To a degree it is likely to be related with historical factors, that *Path Dependency* once again. Thus, countries that arguably were exploited by colonies like Indonesia, Kenya and Gabon have high scores on the multiculturalism index (eighty and above). They were artificial creations established along lines drawn by the imperialist powers. Conversely, the former colonial countries in the West, like France, the Netherlands and Britain, have relatively homogeneous populations. But this still does not explain why multicultural states fare so poorly. The somewhat lazy assumption that these countries lacked cohesion, and the observation that they tend to fall apart if they do not have a *Staatsvolk* does not explain the crucial question why.

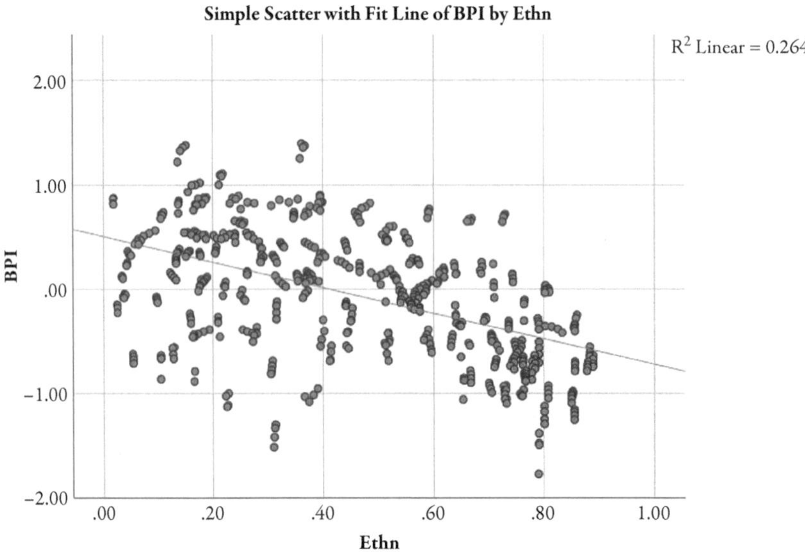

Figure 3.16 BPI and Ethnic Fractionalisation

Here we have to digress to understand the logic. The traditional argument, at least among historical sociologists, is that societies were organised around natural small communities before the industrial age. In these small societies there was a natural cohesion, or what the sociologist Emile Durkheim called a 'mechanical solidarity'; everybody knew one-another and would care for their neighbours[57]. But more people moved to cities to work in factories. Hence, the natural sense of community evaporated and something had to be put in its stead. The actual community had to be replaced with an 'imagined community', an invented sense of solidarity that would prompt people to feel commonality with – and literally compassion for – fellow citizens they didn't know[58]. The answer to this was nationalism. Though in a different sense than we perhaps know today.

Certain politicians – those of the nationalist right – will tell you that nations have always existed that there is a soul of the people that harks back to the beginning of time. In fact, the word nation was hardly used at all before the French Revolution. For all intents and purposes, 'nationalism was an ideology invented at the beginning of the 19th Century'[59]. What is now often associated with tattooed skinheads and flag-waving and overweight white men, was once a means of creating social solidarity. When the philosopher Rousseau was advising the Polish government on a new constitution, he had a clear sense that his cherished model of the local community was dying. In his philosophical works the Genevan born thinker had eulogised the small city-state where everybody gathered in the town square to discuss matters, and where and where everyone fell a natural kinship with their neighbours. But from his travels he could see that this society was becoming obsolete. When the facts change, you must change your mind. Rousseau realised that it was necessary to create a new sense of community and unity through education, and 'shape the souls of the citizens in a national pattern, and so direct their opinions, their likes, and their dislikes so that they shall be patriotic by inclination, passionately, of necessity'[60].

57 Emile Durkheim (1911). *De la division du travail social*. Paris F. Alcan.

58 Benedict Anderson (2006). *Imagined Communities: Reflections on the Origin and Spread of Nationalism*. London: Verso Books.

59 Elie Kedouri (1960) *Nationalism*. Oxford: Blackwell, p. 1.

60 Jean-Jacques Rousseau, (1964) 'Considérations sur le gouvernement de Pologne' *Oeuvres Complétes III*. Paris. *Bibliothèque de la Pléiade*, pp. 951–1041, p. 966.

Rousseau knew this patriotism was not natural and that it had to be invented for the sake of unity. As he wrote elsewhere, 'while establishing a government for the nation is undoubtedly useful, it is even more useful to establish a nation for the government'. For 'national character' is the most import thing for a state, 'every nation must have one, and if she lacks it we must start by endowing her with it'[61]. To achieve this, the philosopher was rather innovative in his suggestions. While he acknowledged that literature and other elements of high culture were important, his main recommendation was that 'games, festivities and ceremonies' would create solidarity like Bull fights in Spain had done[62].

So, the politicians who faced the challenge of the new impersonal society; the one who witnessed the dying away of old communities, wanted to – and succeeded in – inventing the 'nation', where you would feel solidarity and kinship even with people you had never met, merely because they belonged to (an invented) community.

At the elite level, it was recognised that the invention of nations was a bit of a con. '*L'Italia è fatta. Restano da fare gli italiani*' – roughly translated 'We have made Italy. Now we must make Italians'. Thus, wrote the Italian politician Massimo d'Azeglio one of the statesmen who helped to unify the different states into Italy in 1870. At that time the common people in 'each region, and even the intellectual elite, spoke their mutually unintelligible dialects, and lacked the least vestiges of national consciousness'[63]. But the Italians were created, and with them a sense of solidarity and of caring with other people. Or more precisely, with other Italians.

61 Jean-Jacques Rousseau (1964) 'Projet de constitution pour la Corse' in Oeuvres *Complétes* III. Paris. *Bibliothèque de la Pléiade,* 899–950, at p. 901.

62 Rousseau, 'Considérations sur le gouvernement de Pologne' p. 962.

63 D. Mack Smith (1960) 'Italy' In J. P. T. Bury (editor) *The New Cambridge Modern History, Vol. 10: The Zenith of European Power, 1830–70*. Cambridge: Cambridge University Press, p. 552.

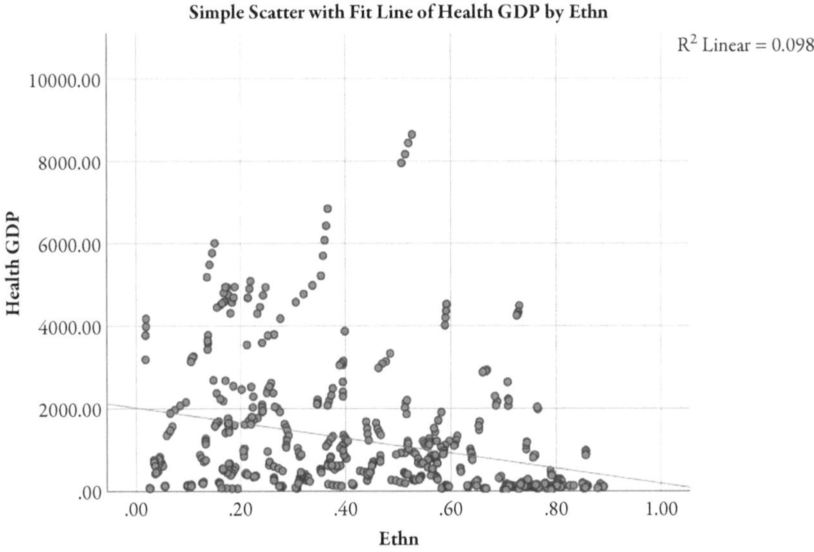

Figure 3.17 Health Care Spending and Ethnic Fractionalisation

In the states that exist today, the same sense of solidarity is still necessary for keeping the countries together. No state can exist without solidarity. And invented or not – appeals to a common culture, a common history – and even a common football team – creates a sense of unity. That ethnic fractionalisation is negatively correlated with a high score on the better place index, is, therefore, to be expected. And, it is even more telling that there is less spending on health in countries with many different ethnic groups. Paying for other people's health care and investing in more hospitals and more doctors to care for people you don't know, is more likely when you feel a sense of kinship with these unknown compatriots. The graph (Figure 3.16) shows that more ethnic diversity is negatively correlated with more public spending on health (the correlation is a negative -32). And, there are similar tendencies between the number of hospital beds and ethnic diversity (a negative correlation of -36) and likewise for the proportion of doctors and multinational populations (a correlation of -40).

So, plainly heterogeneous populations have negative drawbacks. Is that just a fact of life? Is it just a sociological law that different peoples cannot live prosperously together? Not entirely. As the figure also shows there are outliers; places that have a high level of multiculturalism and yet do well on the Better Place Index, and on other measures. How is this possible and are there things that can be learned?

For example, Switzerland – the country that has been in first place on the Better Place Index every single year since 2010 – is famously a country comprised by different religious groups and with four official languages. The same is true for other high-scoring countries, such as the very diverse Singapore, Belgium and Canada.

In the years after the Second World War, when sociologists and political scientists began to speculate about these matters, they too reached the agreement that diversity was likely to lead to the breakdown of countries. It was only when these differences were blunted by other factors, such as religion or class, that divided societies could prosper. By belonging to different groups, ethnicity would be less of a problem. A poor Irish person in England would feel solidarity with impoverished English workers and have more in common with class comrades than with a prosperous compatriot, to use but one example.

But the problem was that some countries were successful even when class, religion and ethnicity overlapped. In Switzerland the Calvinists were richer than the Catholics, but they also belonged to a different ethnic group and were French as opposed to German speakers. Likewise, in Finland, the Swedish speakers were prosperous, whereas those who spoke *Suomi* were poorer. So how can these countries be successful? What accounts for their prosperity and the generally favourable outcomes?

When looked at more closely, these countries have something in common; political power-sharing. With an unhelpful – and virtually unpronounceable – term, social scientists have called it 'consociationalism'. What characterise these countries is that they have learned to agree to disagree[64]. This means that different communities are allowed to govern their own affairs, have their own schools and universities, and even different hospitals. In the Netherlands, a country that was as divided between

64 Arend Lijphart (1968) *The Politics of Accommodation: Pluralism and Democracy in the Netherlands*. Berkeley CA: University of California Press, p. 124.

richer Protestants and poorer Catholics as Northern Ireland across the sea, the two groups agreed in the nineteenth century to set up a system of so-called *Zuilen*, literally pillars. Those from the protestant tradition would start their education in a Calvinist Kindergarten, move on to a protestant school, work in a cooperative or for an employer who shared their own religious persuasion, before he or she would retire to a Calvinist nursery home, and finally be laid to rest on the cemetery of the Dutch Reformed Church. He or she would have very few connections with Catholics. The only thing that would keep the country together would be power-sharing between the elites – the leaders of each of the religious communities. These would form a coalition government and share the burdens necessary for paying for the schools, a civil service, and of course build dikes to defend the country from flooding from the North Sea[65].

The same system existed in Switzerland, where 'Catholics not only had their own party, they also had the own trade unions, newspapers, and bookshops'[66]. But, like the Dutch, the Swiss were not always accommodating, nor did they accept the national and religious differences that existed.

After a war between the Catholic cantons (the so-called *Sonderbund*) in 1847, the Swiss political system gradually took on the characteristics of a 'consociational' society after 1920 when a system of proportional representation meant that all the different religious and ethnic groups could get representation in the federal legislature, and the system took on its present form after 1958 when the four largest parties formed a permanent coalition government of the Liberals, the Christian Democratic Party, the Socialists and the conservative People's Party. This arrangement is not a marriage of love but one of toleration, and often thorny issues are submitted to referendums. This feature allows the Swiss Parties to concurrently appeal to their core voters and at the same time continue to work pragmatically together.

Statistically, heterogeneous and diverse societies rarely work, but through a fortunate set of political institutions the Dutch and still more

65 Lijphart, *The Politics of Accommodation,* p. 115.

66 Wolf Lindner (2010) *Swiss Democracy: Possible Solutions to Conflict in Multicultural Societies*. London: Palgrave, p. 22.

the Swiss were able to forge societies that were exceptionally successful despite being profoundly divided.

So maybe the countries ranked in the top end of the Better Place Index are not just rich because of the weather, their religion (or rather lack there-off) but due to other factors and for reasons we *can* do something about. But the question is – and remains –if other countries can change their constitutions and achieve the same success as the Swiss and the Dutch, or if these two European countries were just lucky to strike political gold?

'At the birth of societies, the leaders of republics create the institutions; thereafter, it is the institutions that form the leaders of republics,' wrote Montesquieu – the weather-obsessed Frenchmen we cited at the beginning of this chapter[67]. Perhaps so, but are these *chefs des républiques* able to create institution in the fashion of constitutional engineers, or are institutions just accidents of history that are created by default rather than by design?

What does the data tell us about the forms of government? Should we opt for a democracy? Or, are we better off if have a strong leader? Was the Medieval Italian poet Dante correct when he said that societies fall apart, 'unless there is one ruler who rules over everybody'?[68] The next chapter answers that question.

67 Charles de Secondat Montesquieu, C. L. (1951). 'Considérations sur les causes de la grandeur des Romains et de leur décadence', in Roger Caillois (editor) *Montesquieu: Œuvres Complétes*. Paris Gallimard, p. 70.

68 Dante Alighieri (1996). *Dante: Monarchy*. Cambridge: Cambridge University Press, p. 27.

CHAPTER 4

Politics and Better Place

As we saw at the end of the previous chapter, the author of the *Divine Comedy* lauded government by one man. One of the poet's contemporary compatriots was equally unquestioning in his support for the same idea. 'Government by one person is likely to be more successful than government by the many,' opined Saint Thomas Aquinas[1].

But that, of course, was in the middle ages, at a time when everybody believed in fairies and Hell physically located below the ground. In the modern age it has been different. Maybe things just change? Maybe we too are prejudiced and accept the prevailing view without bothering to look at the evidence? Since the Second World War it has been difficult to find anyone who would stand up for rule by one man or an unelected clique. Even a state like North Korea is officially called 'The People's Republic of Korea', though the role of the 'people' – let alone the voters – is absent in the totalitarian state.

And, yet, the unquestioned opposition against authoritarianism has slightly changed after the Millennium. In Britain, one of the world's longest established democracies, 54 percent want 'a strong leader who is willing to break the rules' – only 23 percent do not[2]. Further, the Australians, an egalitarian people devoted to the classless idea of 'mateship', are increasingly in favour of a 'strong man'. While the hankering for a benevolent despot is not as high as in the United Kingdom, no less than 33 percent of Australians rated having an authoritarian style of leader as being 'very

1 Thomas Aquinas (1959) 'De Regimine Principum', in A. P. D'Entreves (Editor) *Aquinas Selected Writings*. Oxford: Basil Blackwell, pp. 2–83, at p. 11.

2 According to the Hansard Society. This is based on this organisation's annual survey. <https://www.hansardsociety.org.uk/publications/reports/audit-of-political-engagement-16>. Accessed 29 March 2020.

good' or 'fairly good' in a recent survey. Ten years before, the number was ten percent lower[3].

Even intellectuals are coming around to the idea. A book aptly entitled *Against Democracy* railed 'against democratic triumphalism', and the author went on to ask – somewhat rhetorically, 'what kind of value does democracy have – if any?'[4]. The question remained unanswered in the book, but others have helpfully found that, authoritarian states may not always be a good idea. For example, 'all international wars since World War I have involved dictatorships. Two-Thirds of civil wars and ethnic conflicts since World War II have erupted in countries under authoritarian rule'. And, yet, at the same time, 'the fastest growing countries in the world are dictatorships'. Perhaps the 40 percent of the world's countries that are ruled by an authoritarian regime are more successful – despite their tendency to go to war[5]. This, once again, is a factual question, one that can be answered by data and evidence and not by selected examples.

So far, we have looked at the economics and the sociology of success. We have established that high levels of taxation and a high number of immigrants lead to higher scores on the Better Place Index. We have also found that religion is negatively correlated with success. So, could it be that states governed by a small and competent elite are better at providing better results and are more successful?

The fundamental question is simple and straightforward: do dictatorships perform better?

Needless to say, to answer this question we need a definition. Those who do nothing but study these types of regimes say they are characterised by 'the absence of fair, reasonably competitive elections through which citizens choose who make policies on their behalf'[6]. Another way of measuring thee regimes is to use the so-called *Freedom House Index*, which has categorised different regimes according to the transparency and fairness

3 <https://www.anu.edu.au/news/all-news/support-for-authoritarian-leaders-in-australia-on-the-rise>

4 Jason Brennan (2016) *Against Democracy*. Princeton, NJ: Princeton University Press, p. 6 and p. 204.

5 Barbara Geddes, Joseph Wright and Erica Frantz (2018) *How Dictatorships Work: Power, Personalization, and Collapse*. Cambridge University Press, pp. 1–2.

6 Barbara Geddes et al. *How Dictatorships Work*, p. 1.

(or otherwise) of electoral processes since 1973. Both seem to make sense and will be used in the following. But we need to be open to different interpretations and possibilities so we will measure dictatorship in different ways. The aim overall is to be fair and keep an open mind, and not be swayed by lazy assumptions – even if this means that we may on occasion reach conclusions which are controversial and uncomfortable.

But first, let's get a bit of background to get us started. It is always a good idea to see what people have thought about this matter. In the Middle Ages the famous philosopher Saint Thomas Aquinas – and he was not the only one – felt that too many decision-makers would make everything messy. 'It is clear', wrote the Saint, 'that many persons will never succeed in producing unity … so it is better for one to rule rather than many who must reach agreement first.'[7] For some people just know more than other people, so why not let the insightful govern? So, why not have those with insight make the decisions?

To take the view that it is better to let the wise decide is not just a medieval preference. Throughout history, many people – philosophers and (not surprisingly) Kings – have taken the same view. Josef II, the Austrian Emperor at the end of the 1700s, summed up the official philosophy of government by a single individual in the words: *Alles für das Volk, aber nichts durch das Volk* – 'Everything for the people but nothing by the people'[8].

A few years later, French Revolution challenged this and for a brief period, there was something approaching 'government by the people' in Europe. After the storm of the Bastille, the French revolutionaries enacted a very liberal constitution – they even decriminalised homosexuality and gave civil rights to the Jews.

But the revolution turned sour and ended in a tyranny and the bloodshed that killed Josef II's sister. (The Austrian emperor was the older brother of the unfortunate Marie Antoinette, the Queen of France who was executed in 1793). Even many who had previously hailed it, like the English poet William Wordsworth who, in 1789, had greeted the Revolution with the words, 'Bliss was it in that dawn to be alive'[9], now warned against

7 Aquinas, 'De Regimine Principum', p. 11.

8 <https://www.habsburger.net/de/kapitel/der-nuetzliche-kaiser-joseph-ii>. Accessed 20 April 2020.

9 Wordsworth, Ibid.

'democracy'. The writer shuddered at the thought that ordinary people could be given the vote and warned that if 'the pot-house keepers of our overgrown manufacturing towns and enormous cities had each and all been invested with the right of voting, the infection would spread like a plague'. In short government by the people would be 'the greatest political evil that could befall the land'[10]. So, enthusiasm for democracy nosedived and intellectuals once again came around to the (alleged) benefits of government by a single man. A textbook for students of law at the *University of Berlin* from 1821 told the future lawyers that 'the idea that all should participate in the business of the state … [was] a ridiculous notion'[11]. To have a monarch, the writer of the textbook wrote simply, was 'an expression of rationality'[12]. One of the law students who used the book was named Karl Marx. The man who went on to write the *Communist Manifesto* had but scorn for liberal democracy: 'Any state after a revolution requires a dictatorship – and an energetic one at that.'[13]

This idea still has many followers. In the People's Republic of China, so-called *Xi Jinping Thought* is based on the idea that increased prosperity is a result of the (allegedly) wise stewardship of the Communist Party. President Xi, not surprisingly, has said that the philosophy of Karl Marx remains 'totally correct'[14].

But, of course, a quote does not establish a fact. So, what are the facts?

This is easier said than done. Dictatorships – or autocratic states – come in different shapes and sizes. Some are one-party states like the People's Republic of China and Vietnam (they tend to be bigger) are based on hierarchical and rationalised bureaucracies and claim legitimacy from their ability to govern efficiently – and sprinkle this with reference to ideological

10 William Wordsworth (2009) [1818] 'Two Addresses to the Freeholders of Westmoreland', in W. J. B Owen (Editor) *Wordsworth's Political Writings*. Penrith Humanities-Ebooks, pp. 279–373, at 335–336.

11 G. W. F. Hegel (2008) *Outlines of the Philosophy of Right*. Oxford: Oxford University Press, p. 295.

12 Hegel, *Philosophy of Right*, p. 258.

13 Karl Marx (1959) 'Die Krisis und die Kontrerevolution', in *Karl Marx - Friedrich Engels – Werke*, Vol. 5. Dietz Verlag, Berlin/DDR 1959, pp. S. 398–404, at 402.

14 <https://uk.reuters.com/article/uk-germany-marx-china/no-regrets-xi-says-marxism-still-totally-correct-for-china-idUKKBN1I50F1>

slogans. By contrast, active monarchies like the ones in the Gulf States, which tend to be smaller, are governed by families and rely on respect for tradition. To compare these two would be too blunt as they operate in very different ways. So, let's begin with the smaller monarchies.

Active Monarchies

The active monarchies are typically states like Saudi Arabia, Kuwait and the United Arab Emirates – but also Bhutan – which through the accidents of history and clever statesmanship have maintained their system of government at a time in history when democracy became the norm. Power politics – or narrow interest played a part. For example, when the British left Qatar in 1971 they were relaxed about the complete lack of democratic structures in a system that was ruled by the Emir Sheik Khalifa bin Hamad. Having a bridgehead in the Gulf and a steady supply of oil was more important at this stage in the Cold War than idealistic principles. Whether matters have changed much is for the reader to reflect on.

That many of the absolute monarchies have natural resources might give them an unfair advantage and the system of government might have little to do with their wealth and (perhaps) general success. Yet, as we saw in Chapter 1 while these countries are generally wealthy, they do not get a high score on the Better Place Index. But again, we only looked at a few examples. What are the general tendencies?

There is a slight tendency that active monarchies are wealthier, but the correlation is below the threshold of 20 percent, and cannot be regarded as significant in any way. There is no correlation neither better nor worse when it comes to, respectively infant mortality or life expectancy. But there is a considerable negative correlation between active monarchies and CO_2 emissions of just below -41 percent.

The countries that are governed by an absolute monarch have a tendency to have fewer hospital beds (the correlation is -22). Many of these countries have draconian penal codes. For example, in Saudi Arabia homicide the category of so-called *Qisas* – a type of offences that are punished by *eye-for-an-eye* retaliatory punishments – are positively medieval; in 2018 a man was crucified after he was accused of stabbing his wife to death[15]. A few figures can put the legal system in the Kingdom in further perspective. Between July 2017 and February 2018, there were 133 public executions in Saudi Arabia (on average 16.6 a month), compared with 67 between October 2016 and May 2017 (on average 8.4 a month). Most of the executions were by beheading[16]. While Saudi Arabia has more executions than its neighbours, there are similar forms of draconian executions in similar states. The United Arab Emirates, like her larger neighbour, also uses stoning as a form of punishment. Without a confession or direct proof, as the newspaper *Khaleej Times* nonchalantly reported, 'two Asian women who committed adultery and got pregnant out of wedlock have been given capital punishment in two separate cases by the Abu Dhabi Criminal Court of First Instance'[17]. Yet despite these harsh punishments, there is *nothing* that suggests that these countries have significantly lower levels of homicide. There is *no correlation* between the murder rate and living in an active monarchy. Nor is there a correlation between these types of traditionalist states and the score on the Better Place Index. While monarchies are not entirely unsuccessful – for example, they have marginally lower unemployment and inflation rates – they hardly provide a model for other countries to emulate.

One-Party States

But these types of traditionalist societies are miles apart from the political systems of China, Vietnam and Cuba. Based on a Marxist-Leninist ideology – officially at least – these states are based on what Lenin (the

15 <https://www.bloomberg.com/news/articles/2018-08-08/saudi-arabia-carries-out-rare-crucifixion-for-murder-theft>. Accessed 9 July 2020.

16 <https://www.bbc.co.uk/news/uk-43316987>. Accessed 9 July 2020.

17 <https://www.khaleejtimes.com/nation/crime/two-women-sentenced-to-death-for-adultery>. Accessed 13 July 2020.

founder of the Soviet Union) called 'democratic centralism'. The idea espoused by the Russian revolutionary was that the 'Vanguard' of the Communist Party – those with expertise and insight – should call the shots. In the original version of this type of society, the leaders would be elected by the *Soviets* – the councils of workers and soldiers, who in turn would be chosen by the people at large[18]. Such a system, the Soviet revolutionary argued, would be based on expertise and science. Lenin himself was enamoured by American so-called *scientific management*. In the late nineteenth century the American engineer Frederick Taylor had invented the first models on how to optimise workflows, which became associated with him name. His idea put crudely was that the management should break down every action, job, or task into small and simple segments which can be easily analysed and taught. In this way there could be targets and people could be rewarded for their performance. While Lenin was – of course – dismissive of capitalism in general, he became very keen on *Taylorism*, provided a recipe for 'the greatest scientific achievements in the field of analysing mechanical motions during work'. In Lenin's view, 'the Soviet Republic must at all costs adopt all that is valuable in the achievements of science and technology in this field'[19].

This pragmatic and evidence-based approach to governance was not just a characteristic of the earliest communists. President Xi of China cited 'scientific management' as key in one of his speeches[20]. The important thing here – interesting though it is – is not that that Chinese President said that 'to dismiss Lenin and Stalin … is to engage in historic nihilism'[21] – rather the important thing is that the (largely) communist states are willing to and even encourage a 'scientific' approach to government, which is not based on tradition, like in the case of the absolute monarchies.

18 V. I. Lenin (1965) 'Report on the Unity Congress of the R.S.D.L.P.' *Lenin: Collected Works,* Vol. 10. Moscow: Progress Publishers, pp. 317–382.

19 V. I. Lenin (1972) 'The Immediate Tasks of the Soviet Government', in *Lenin's Collected Work,* Vol. 27. Moscow: Progress Publishers, pp. 235–277, p. 240.

20 <https://www.scmp.com/comment/opinion/article/3013620/china-must-heed-xi-call-tackling-waste>. Accessed 9 July 2020.

21 Xi Jinping quoted in <https://chinadigitaltimes.net/2013/01/leaked-speech-shows-xi-jinpings-opposition-to-reform/>. Accessed 9 July 2020.

So, does it make a difference? Are the one-party states successful? These countries have a slight tendency to have lower levels of unemployment (though not to a degree that statisticians would find acceptable). Statistically speaking, one-party states are not associated with either higher or lower inequality, nor with more doctors per 10,000 citizens. There is simply no correlation either way. The same is true for one-party states' economic performance. And, if anything, there is the tiniest of tendencies towards a negative association between these states and GDP per Capita, just as there is a microscopic tendency that countries with a one-party state have a lower BPI.

While one-party states are not associated with more pollution, there is no suggestion that having a system of 'democratic centralism' – or Xi Jinping thought – is associated with lower CO_2 emissions.

In recent years, China has presented its model as one to be emulated. A Chinese Professor expressed this in these words, 'So long as the American model remains unable to deliver the desired outcome, as shown so clearly in failures from Haiti to the Philippines to Iraq, the Chinese model will become more appealing to the world's poor'[22]. Whether the American model is attractive will be dealt with below.

Overall, the case for autocratic countries, namely that they have rapid growth and the argument that they provide better government outcomes, is not supported by facts. The so-called *allure of the Chinese model* that some talked about a few years back, and which is a central part of the People's Republic's official foreign policy, is not convincing, and certainly not supported by statistics.

But, admittedly, there are relatively few one-party states. This makes it difficult to carry out statistical analysis. There need to be a minimum number of cases to make sure the data is representative. If there are too few cases, the margin of error – as professionals call it – is too great to draw meaningful conclusions.

22 *Wei-Wei Zhang* (2006) 'The allure of the Chinese model', *International Herald Tribune*, 1 Nov A10.

Competitive Autocracies

But maybe we are looking in the wrong places. Maybe it is obsolete to look at one-party states and active monarchies? Some of the scholars who have written about non-democratic regimes have noted that many of them – on the surface at least – seem to look like democracies, whereas in reality they are not. The experts' not always helpful – and slightly confusing term for these types of states – is *competitive authoritarianism*[23].

For example, in Azerbaijan there are eleven different parties represented in the *Milli Məclis* – the national assembly. There are elections using a system of proportional representation and a political model that looks very much like that of France; a so-called *semi-presidential* system with a directly elected president and a prime minister who needs the support of a majority in the legislature. (We shall talk more about these kinds of systems later in this chapter). And, yet despite this, the party *Yeni Azərbaycan Partiyası* always wins a majority of the seats. The president comes from the same party, and so far, he has also come from the same family. The current President Ilham Aliyev is the son of Heydar Aliyev – the first president after the fall of communism. And, to make this story of the family firm complete, the younger Aliyev served as prime minister before he succeeded his father.

Such as system is difficult to categorise. Azerbaijan (and countries like it) are not classic dictatorships in the mould of caricature totalitarian state or the tinpot tyrant type; rather 'democratic procedures are sufficiently meaningful for opposition groups to take them seriously as arenas through which to contest for power. It is just that they never win unless foreign powers intervene or unless the autocratic leaders fall out with each other as happened in Sudan, Malaysia or Zimbabwe[24]. When scholars categorise almost half of the world's states as authoritarian, it is because most look

23 Steven Levitsky and Lucan A. Way (2010) *Competitive Authoritarianism: Hybrid Regimes after the Cold War*. Cambridge: Cambridge University Press.

24 Levitsky and Way *Competitive Authoritarianism*, p. 7.

like Azerbaijan: 'Dictatorships increasingly rely on pseudo-democratic institutions.'[25]

The set-up is the same in Russia, Cambodia and the Democratic Republic of Congo[26]. In the latter, for example, there are sixteen parties in the *Assemblée nationale*; officially power is shared by a prime minister and a president – exactly as in Azerbaijan. It is just that power never really changes hands as a result of an election. The current president Félix Tshisekedi admittedly won an election, but he was only able to contest it because powerful interests in neighbouring countries withdrew support from Joseph Kabila, who had inherited the presidency from his father Laurent eighteen years before.

In some ways this masquerade is nothing new. After the Caesars dismantled the Roman Republic around the year 30 BCE, in the Roman historian Suetonius, observed in how the emperor – on the face of it – democratised the Roman state, 'by granting city councillors of the colonies the right to vote', and even how 'ballots were placed and sealed in containers and counted at Rome on polling day'[27]. And yet, as another, more critical historian of the same vintage, noted, the emperor, 'gradually pushed ahead and absorbed the functions of the senate, the officials and even the law'[28].

Such façade systems are difficult to be subject to statistical scrutiny, and the members of parliaments, for rather obvious reasons, are unwilling to speak out. Yet the little evidence there is reinforces the impression of rubber-stamp institutions with no power whatsoever. For example, in Jordan, only seven percent of the deputies thought parliament played a large role[29]. Similarly, in Indonesia, during the thirty-one years of dictatorship under Suharto, legislative assembly 'never drafted its own legislation and never rejected a bill submitted by the executive branch, [and] had no say in Cabinet appointments', despite what the constitution formally said[30].

25 Barbara Geddes et al. *How Dictatorships Work*, p. 139.

26 Steven Levitsky and Lucan A. Way (2002) 'Elections without Democracy: The Rise of Competitive Authoritarianism', *Journal of Democracy*, 13(2), 51–65.

27 Suetonius (2007) *The Twelve Caesars*. London: Penguin, p. 71.

28 Tacitus (1986) *The Annals of Imperial Rome*. London: Penguin, p. 32.

29 Barbara Geddes et al. *How Dictatorships Work*, p. 137.

30 Adam Schwarz (2000) *A Nation in Waiting*. London: Routledge, p. 272.

The Soviet dictator Joseph Stalin is said to have noted that 'what matters is not who votes, but who counts the ballots'. In the 1930s several Western observers were duped by this and did not realise that in many autocratic states, formal political institutions and rights are mere words. *The Constitution (Fundamental law) of the Union of Soviet Socialist Republics 1936* guaranteed 'a) freedom of speech; b) freedom of the press; c) freedom of assembly, including the holding of mass meetings; [and] d) freedom of street processions and demonstrations', at a time when millions were carried off to the *Gulag Camps*, and stipulated that (Art. 32) 'the legislative power of the U.S.S.R. is exercised exclusively by the Supreme Soviet of the U.S.S.R.', at a time when Josef Stalin's word was law.

That states that look like democracies are not, suggests that we need a more nuanced way of measuring authoritarian states. And such a measure exists[31]. As noted above, the American think tank Freedom House has published a ranking of countries according to the fairness (or often otherwise) of their elections[32]. Basically, theirs is a measure of democracy. Based on this, it is possible to make a simple correlation between the two factors; democracy (as calculated by Freedom House) and the BPI-score and test

31 In fact, there are a whole range of measures. Another famous one is *PolityIV* and there is a measure developed by the magazine *The Economist.*

32 The Freedom House Score is based on assessments on whether a country holds (1) Competitive, multiparty political system; if there is (2) Adult suffrage for all citizens without criminal convictions (some states may further punish and subjugate people with criminal convictions by disenfranchising them from the democratic process); If (3) These regularly contested elections are conducted in conditions of ballot secrecy, reasonable ballot security, and the absence of massive voter fraud that yields results that are unrepresentative of the public will; and (4) If there is significant public access of major political parties to the electorate through the media and through generally open political campaigning. Based on expert assessments, which can be criticised, for a country to be categorised as an electoral democracy, it must score seven or more out of twelve in political rights subcategory A (Electoral Progress), and have an overall aggregate score of twenty in their political rights rating and an overall aggregate score of thirty in their civil liberties rating. See <https://freedomhouse.org/reports/freedom-world/freedom-world-research-methodology>.

The Freedom House Score is largely based on expert assessments, which – as outlined in Chapter 1, can be criticised. On this see: Kenneth A. Bollen (1986) 'Political Rights and Political Liberties in Nations: An Evaluation of Human Rights Measures, 1950 to 1984'. *Human Rights Quarterly,* 8(4), 567–591.

the proposition that authoritarian regimes do better and are more successful. So, are they?

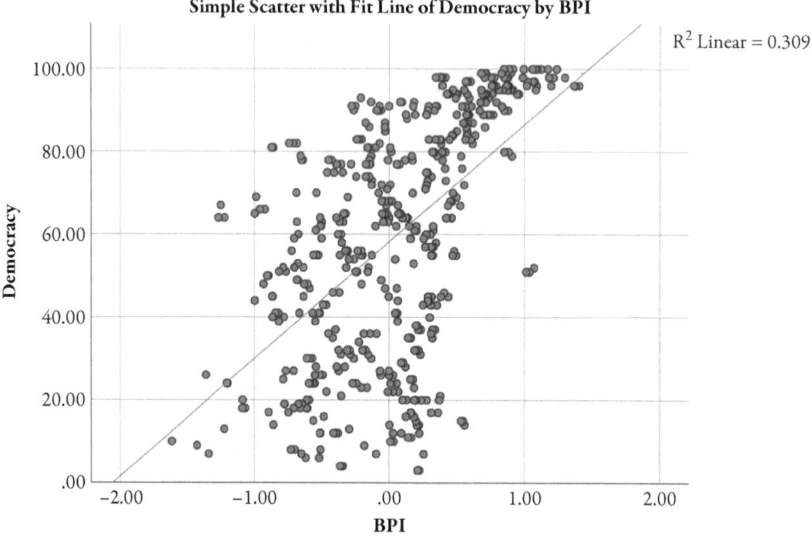

Figure 4.1 Democracy and the Better Place Index

Overall, there are many things that do not get better in authoritarian states. For every notch up the Freedom House scale, there are 0.5 percent fewer murders. Similarly, a one-point drop on the same index is associated with a net loss of $297 per citizen. There is a 44 percent negative correlation between dictatorship and economic output. Given this, it is hardly surprising that there is a whopping -56 negative correlation between authoritarian states and the Better Place Index.

This correlation is unambiguous and is exceptionally high for the social sciences. Basically the claim regarding the superiority of non-democratic states that 'the best form of government is that which is carried out by one person', as Thomas Aquinas said, is not supported[33].

33 Thomas Aquinas (1959) 'Summa Theologica', in A. P. D'Entreves (Editor) *Aquinas Selected Writings*. Oxford: Basil Blackwell, pp. 103–179, at p. 107.

We can also show this relationship in another way. For example, following the likes of President Xi in China, we would expect countries that are categorised as 'democracies' by Freedom House to do worse than countries that are not. This can be tested very easily. Put bluntly, countries that score over fifty on the Freedom House index are (to varying degrees) 'democracies'. Countries that fall below this threshold are not. So how do they fare?

Once again, the results do not support the authoritarians. Countries in the 'democracies' bracket have a BPI of, on average, 0.19. Countries that are, to varying degrees, authoritarian, by contrast, have a BPI average of -0.27.

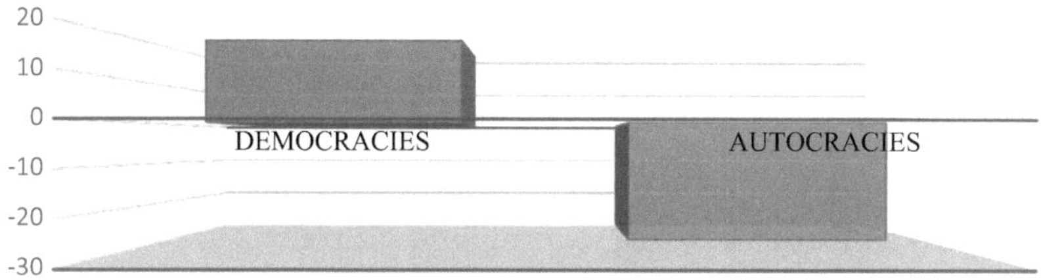

Figure 4.2 Average BPI in Democracies and Autocracies

And, if we want to focus on the economic side of things, countries categorised as democracies also have markedly higher average GDP per Capita than the countries that are not democracies. The difference is stark – at just over $17K. The former countries have an average that is more than $10,000 higher than non-democracies.

Figure 4.3 Average GDP per Capita in Democracies and Non-Democracies (in US Dollars)

All this, naturally, begs the question, why do dictatorships not work? Why is it that human societies do not work, when people are told what to do? There are several theories – many of them well substantiated. We start with Kleptocracy.

Why Are Dictatorships Unsuccessful?

For starters, being a dictator is not quite as easy as one might think. We can get an illustration of this from Ghana.

In a previous incarnation I had a job in Africa. It was at the military academy in Accra in Ghana, right next to a mango grove, though they never produced any mangoes – not for sale anyway. Why was it there? My colleague, a charismatic military man with a barytone voice, gave me nonchalant explanation: 'Well, it was one of the things, our leader Kwame Nkrumah, had to concede. You see, the commander wanted to grow mangos, so the President gave the land to him in return for his support. But he was a great man! He made the country great.' My colleague was, somewhat exotically in these parts, named Vladimir, after the founder of the Soviet Union. 'I was born in the year when Nkrumah was awarded the *Lenin Peace Prize*,' he told me with ill-disguised pride.

No doubt, Nkrumah had charisma, a legendary African statesman, the first president of the independent Ghana in the 1960s. He had charm too. Princess Margaret invited him to dance parties at *Buckingham Palace* with the Queen and Prince Philip. But Nkrumah ruled as an absolute – if mostly benevolent – dictator. However, he was not all-powerful. He needed the support of other prominent individuals. Kwame Nkrumah realised that the 'strongman' always has to be on the look-out for enemies, even among his closest allies and friends. That is why the Ghanean strongman had to placate the army commander and give him an orchard. Again, this is nothing new. 'Plots against despots as often as not are the work of those who profess the deepest affection for them,' said the Greek tyrant Hiero over

2300 years ago[34]. Thus, the despot – whether in ancient Greece, in Ghana in the 1960s, or in Azerbaijan in the twenty-first century – is distracted from the business of governing because he fears he will be overthrown.

And the longer the dictatorship lasts, the more enemies the tyrant will get, and the more desperate he becomes. The real problem in a dictatorship is that most despots are faced with the same problem as Kwame Nkrumah: to secure continued support from other powerful people lest they should find a better offer. As discontent wells up, those in powerful positions (generals, rich men and influential individuals) will demand an ever-increasing price for their loyalty. When protests began in Venezuela in the 2010s, President Maduro increased pay to the military. Gradually, as the discontent rose, the top brass of the army in the oil-rich but impoverished Latin American country increased ten-fold while pay for hospital doctors decreased by the same proportion[35].

Some have even seen tendencies in this direction within the European Union. Viktor Orbán, the Hungarian prime minister, has been accused of 'siphoning off tens of millions of pounds' under a system that English conservative newspaper *The Times* called 'legalised corruption'[36].

The Economist, another widely trusted publication with a centre-right political preference, wrote about how Orbán, to placate local elites paid for a football stadium, which 'cost a fortune' and a 'tourist train', which 'runs half-empty most of the time'. Like in Ghana and Venezuela, 'Kleptocratic elites bleed public services while *Fidesz*, the ruling party, chips away at Hungary's democracy'[37].

The aim of this chapter is not to make a moral judgement on dictatorship, but merely to show that the economic case for this system of

34 Xenophon (1968) 'Hiero', Translated by E. C. Merchant in Xenophon: Scripta Minora, Cambride, MA: Harvard University Press, pp. 1–57, at p. 17.

35 The Times, 'Venezuela's Maduro buys loyalty of military amid coup fears', 18 July 2018.

36 The Times 'Czech and Hungarian Leaders "siphoning-off millions" in EU Funds', *The Times*, 5 November.

37 *The Economist*, 'The EU is tolerating – and enabling – authoritarian Kleptocracy in Hungary', 5 April 2018.

government is found wanting. The money that is channelled to pointless projects to keep potential challengers sweet, costs vast sums, which could otherwise have been spent on improving the livelihood of the many. 'Under absolutist political institutions,' the economists Daron Acemoglu and James Robinson concluded, 'those who can wield this power will be able to set up economic institutions to enrich themselves and augment their power at the expense of society.'[38]

Like Kwame Nkrumah before him, Viktor Orbán, recognise the elementary logic of dictatorship. The autocrats who do not understand the anatomy of authoritarianism will have a short career. To be a policy expert, someone who actually brings prosperity to a country, will not last long in the job unless, he understands the politics of giving handouts to the powerful few. As alluded to, this logic does not only apply to modern day dictators. To be a successful despot, you need to give windfalls to those who can keep you in power. Some were masters of this. Augustus – the first Roman Emperor – was skilled in this art, and as a historian from the time noted, 'he [Augustus] seduced the army with bonuses, and his cheap food policy was successful bait'[39].

Other historical dictators, however, did not read the memo. And they suffered the consequences. Alexandru Cuza (1820–1873), the King of Danubian Principalities – now known as Romania – did not appreciate this. He was, by all accounts, a benevolent and enlightened ruler, but he was not a democrat. Yet, in many ways, he was the model benign despot; someone who was willing to cut corners to get the necessary but difficult policies enacted. Well-educated and with an understanding of economics, agriculture and foreign affairs, he began a series of improvements that included public education and land-reform. This massively improved the backward state of the country. But the policies were not well-received by the landowners. Cuza refused to give handouts to the powerful military and to wealthy aristocrats. After only five years in power he was removed by the

38 Daron Acemoglu and James A. Robinson (2013) *Why Nations Fail: The Origins of Power, Prosperity, and Poverty*. Profile Books, p. 80.

39 Tacitus (2003) *The Annals of Imperial Rome*. London: Penguin, p. 32.

so-called *Monstrous coalition*[40]. Being an expert in policy is less important than keeping the powerful happy – at least if a dictator wants to survive.

Silencing the Wisdom of the Crowds

'My gut tells me more sometimes than anybody else's brain can ever tell me,' a contemporary politician famously said[41]. It is perhaps the defining character of the autocrat – or politicians of a similar ilk – that they have an elevated opinion of themselves, as well as they are thin skinned and, consequently, take unkindly to criticism. Strongmen build their authority on a unique claim to being right. For this reason, those who speak truth unto power fall out of favour with the strongman – or suffer a much worse fate. When the philosopher Seneca criticised Emperor Nero, he was ordered to commit suicide – and duly complied.

But no politicians are universal geniuses who know all policies. Governing is a difficult business. You need facts and the government needs to know what works in order to make the trains run on time, keep the economy ticking and crime low. Fundamentally, 'it is the duty of governments to form the truest opinions they can'[42]. And it is very rare that know-it-all dictators possess all the facts themselves, or that the ruler can objectively be described as 'a very stable genius', as the aforementioned politician called himself. Once more, this is nothing new. A handbook for would-be despots written centuries ago, advised the budding autocrat that he 'should be a constant questioner', and that he should 'let people

40 Danciu, E. T. (2014) Re-flaming the Political Union and Unionists: Local Historical Reading Frontlines. *Revista de Științe Politice. Revue des Sciences Politiques*, (44), 194–202.

41 Donald Trump in an interview with *The Washington Post*, Quoted in Newsweek, 'Donald Trump Says "My Gut Tells Me More Sometimes Than Anybody Else's Brain Can Ever Tell Me"', 27 November 2018.

42 John Stuart Mill (1991) 'On Liberty', in John Gray (Editor) *On Liberty and Other Essays*. Oxford: Oxford University Press, pp. 5–128, at p. 23.

understand that [he was] not offended by the truth'[43]. Very few autocrats have followed this advice.

In most dictatorships the opposite is true. When Li Wenliang, a Chinese doctor, dared to warn about the Coronavirus in late December 2019 he realised that the Chinese Communist Party were 'offended by the truth'. As a conscientious medical practitioner concerned about the well-being of his colleagues, he sent a message to a chat group warning them about the outbreak and urging them to wear protective clothing to avoid infection. The group was monitored by the authorities. Four days later Dr Li was summoned to the *Public Security Bureau* on the charge of 'making false comments' and having 'severely disturbed the social order'. He was forced to sign a letter. He had no choice but to comply. A month later he was dead. The outbreak of COVID-19 provided incontrovertible evidence that he was not making false comments. In fact, if he had been allowed to speak freely, hundreds of thousands of lives could have been spared, and trillions of dollars would have been saved. But speaking truth onto power would have threatened the power of the Chinese Communist Party[44].

This unwillingness to listen to 'facts', even when they will save millions of lives, is the fundamental problem with dictatorships, and perhaps the chief reason they do not work. Autocracies perform worse because they do *not* allow different opinions. When the philosopher John Stuart Mill and his wife Harriet Taylor Mill wrote their famous book *On Liberty*, they wanted above all to tell their readers that the 'only way in which a human being can make some approach to knowing the whole of a subject, is by hearing what can be said about it by persons of every variety of opinion, and studying all modes in which it can be looked at by every character of mind'[45]. All silencing of discussion is an assumption of infallibility. And the evidence shows that dictators and despots are fallible. Democracy

43 Nicolló Machiavelli (1963) *Il Principe*. Turin: Einaudi, pp.117 and 116.

44 <https://www.bbc.co.uk/news/world-asia-china-51364382>. Accessed 8 April 2020.

45 Mill (1991) 'On Liberty', p. 25. While the cover only lists John Stuart as the author, he acknowledged in his autobiography that the book was 'directly and literally our joint production', John Stuart Mill (2018) *Autobiography*. Oxford: Oxford University Press, p. 141.

works. Dictatorship does not. These are not ideological assertions, but empirical facts.

All the President's Men

Many people seem to favour resolute politicians who act rather than talk. Does that mean they are not democrats? Probably not. Many people, when asked the question about a 'strong man', are possibly just thinking of an efficient and no-nonsense political action man. That would seem to be the case in Britain. In this country most people are still in favour of democracy – well over 60 percent – but 42 percent of them nevertheless agree that 'many of the country's problems could be dealt with more effectively if the government didn't have to worry so much about votes in Parliament'[46].

In France in the 1950s there was constant chaos. Between 1947 and 1958 there were over twenty coalition governments. The collapse of the Empire, economic malaise at home and pressure from a strong communist party petrified the political system. Enter Charles de Gaulle. The wartime hero had returned to his home in Colombey-les-Deux-Églises, when the French had adopted a parliamentary system in 1946. In 1958 he was back with a vengeance. The former general was ready to perform the role of strongman in the country's hour of need. But he wanted exceptional powers – albeit with the approval of the people. As he later explained,

> I was convinced that sovereignty belongs to the people, provided they express themselves directly and as a whole. But I refused to accept that [sovereignty] could be parcelled out among the different interests represented by the parties. I found it necessary for the government to derive not from Parliament, in other words the parties but from over and above them, from a leader directly mandated by the nation as a whole[47].

46 <https://www.hansardsociety.org.uk/blog/finding-of-support-for-a-'strong-leader'-helps-provoke-responses-to-2019>. Accessed 30 March 2020.

47 Charles de Gaulle (1971) *Memoirs of Hope:* London: Weidenfeld Nicholson, 6.

The opposition was largely muted, ineffectual and irrelevant. One of his opponents a young politician named François Mitterrand (he later became president himself), called the system established by de Gaulle 'un coup d'État permanent'[48]. So, did it work, did de Gaulle resolve the problems facing France? Or, more to the point? Can a presidential system 'get things done', as many people seem to believe?

In fact, the French system was not as exceptionally 'presidential' as de Gaulle suggested. In a true presidential system, the president is directly elected, selects his own cabinet, regardless of what parliament thinks. The legislature is just there to debate and enact the laws. Such true presidential system is mainly known from the United States, but it is also common in Latin America and African countries. In Europe, only two countries are truly presidential, namely Turkey and Cyprus.

Much as Charles de Gaulle wanted a presidential system, his system was, to use a technical term, 'semi-presidential'[49]. This means that there is both a president and a prime minister. The president has strong powers, especially in foreign affairs, but he does not select a government at will. He chooses a prime minister, but this individual must have the support of a majority of the members in the legislature – or at least the lower chamber where there is a two-chamber parliament. The semi-presidential system is known from Finland and France, and after the fall of the Berlin Wall, four out of the eighteen post-communist countries replicated this system (Lithuania, Poland, Romania and Russia), only one chose a presidential system (Belarus), and thirteen opted for a parliamentary system with the prime minister as a head of government – though sometimes with a ceremonial president.

48 Mitterrand, F. (1964). *Le coup d'état permanent.* Paris: Plon.

49 The term was defined by the political scientist Maurice Duverger. M. Duverger *(1978). Échec au roi. Paris: A. Michel, though it was first used by the journalist* Hubert Beuve-Méry in an article in *Le Monde* in January 1958, in which he described de Gaulle's takeover as 'a temporary dictatorship under a semi-presidential system'. See Beuve-Méry, Hubert (1988 [1958] 'De la dictature temporaire au régime semi-présidentiel' in Dominique Colas (Editor) *Droit, institutions et systèmes politiques.* Paris: Presses Universitaires de France, pp. 533–540.

But we are not in the business of explaining institutions, but to test if they work. Using this distinction this gives us a neat – if perhaps a little crude – measure of the levels of presidentialism. This is how it works; fully presidential systems like the Philippines, Uruguay and Turkey get the score of two; semi-presidential systems get one, and Parliamentary systems get zero. We can then check this list with the BPI-Index.

So, are presidential systems more successful? Not if our index is anything to go by. There is a negative correlation of -0.47 between presidentialism and our index[50]. Basically, the more presidential, the lower the BPI-score. This is not only true for our index. Generally, presidentialism is associated with an array of ills. The average income is lower the more presidential the system is. What is more, life expectancy is shorter under more presidential systems, and education is worse[51].

So, plainly, presidents don't get things done. Why is that? One commonly held theory is that societies do better when you can hold someone to account. In an economic system you can hold a shop or a business to account by not buying their goods if they are of a poor quality. In the political marketplace you can punish a government by not re-electing it.

But the problem in a presidential system is that there are several authorities you can hold to account. But is it to blame the president or Congress? It is difficult to say. "How is … the *nation, to know which boy needs the whipping?" asked* Woodrow Wilson, the twenty-eighth president of the United States, in a critical account of the American system many years before he became a politician[52].

Put in a different way, the system in which the president competes with congress for power dilutes responsibility. Another American politician summed it up with slightly different words: 'The President blames Congress, the Congress blames the President, and the public remains

50 This is the Pearsons Correlation, It is based on a total of 521 cases, and has a margin of error of less than 0.001 percent.

51 Presidentialism is negatively correlated with GDP per Capita: R= -0.38, with years of schooling -0.41, and life expectancy: R: -0.47, all with a margin of error of less than 0.01 percent (All based on a sample of 497 cases).

52 Wilson, W. (1885) *Congressional Government: A Study in American Politics*. Boston: Houghton, pp. 186–187.

confused and disgusted with government in Washington.'[53] Thus, while both the president and Congress name and shame each other, it is difficult for the people or 'the nation' to point the blame finger. As a result, you don't get the rascals out. And bad policies can continue for longer and trust in government goes down.

Sure, but a president would, at least be able to knock heads together in a crisis, wouldn't he? Maybe not. In an emergency you need the most suitable and the most able crisis manager, not whoever happens to be president. In a system where only Parliament is supreme, it is possible to find a better prime minister in a time of extreme crisis. In Britain, it was relatively simple to replace Chamberlain with Churchill in 1940. The same is not the case under presidentialism.

This advantage of the Parliamentary system would not have come as a great surprise to those who have studied presidential systems in earlier epochs. Walter Bagehot, the legendary editor of *The Economist* in the 1860s, saw this ability to find the right person to deal with a crisis to be one of the main problems with presidentialism. 'Under a cabinet constitution at a sudden emergency the people can choose a ruler for the occasion,' but he continued, 'Under a presidential government you can do nothing of the kind. The American government calls itself a government of the supreme people; but at a quick crisis.' Unlike in a parliamentary system, presidential government has 'no elastic element'[54]. After the 9/11 attack on the World Trade Centre in 2001 the American had no choice but to rely on George Bush Jr.

Perhaps, graver still, a system of presidential government is also likely to be characterised by what is known as 'gridlock'. In simple terms, this is when government is paralysed because the president is from a different party than the majority in the legislature. There was gridlock in America when President Clinton was faced with a Congress dominated by the Republicans after the Mid-Term elections in 1994.

53 Treasure Secretary Clarence Douglas Dillon quoted in J. Sundquist (2011) *Constitutional Reform and Effective Government*. Washington, DC: Brookings Institution Press, p. 11.

54 Walter Bagehot (1894) *The English Constitution*. London: Kegan Paul, Trench Trüber & Co Ltd, pp. 29–30.

Of course, some critics of so-called *Big Government* want politicians to do as little as possible. Some even think that a modicum of paralysis is positive thing. The libertarian American thinktank the *Cato Institute* believed that gridlock is laudable as it increases, 'the likelihood that policies will reflect broad, unorganized interests instead of the interests of narrow, organized groups'[55]. Certainly, there is a case to be made for checks on power, but the Cato Institute's argument certainly does not cut any ice with those who favour presidentialism because it is a way 'of getting things done'

Gridlock has consequences. This is best illustrated with an example from the 1980s. Then President Ronald Reagan faced a hostile Congress with a Democrat majority. The result was frustrating for him. Often Reagan's policies would simply not get voted through Congress, and when they did, they came with a considerable price tag. For example, in return for accepting Reagan's tax reform, House Majority Leader Thomas 'Tip' O'Neill Jr, was able to continue expensive welfare policies. The net result was enormous budget deficits that effective sucked money out of the economic system, left less money for investment, to workers' wages, and ultimately to the social welfare. Adjusted for inflation, the federal government deficit increased from $738 billion to a staggering $2.1 trillion – and the USA went from being the largest creditor to being the largest debtor[56].

The former B-movie actor was elected to be a strong leader; it was to be 'Morning again in America'[57], under a decisive president who would cut red tape and reduce the size of government. Business, so Reagan promised, would thrive under his decisive stewardship. In fact, the private sector's share of GDP shrank[58]. The public sector grew bigger – exactly the opposite of what he had promised. Reagan to his credit admitted this and called it the 'greatest disappointment' of his presidency[59].

55 Marcus Ethridge(2011) *'The Case for Gridlock' Policy Analysis No. 672*. Washington, DC: The Cato Institute, p. 1.

56 <https://fred.stlouisfed.org/graph/?g=k977>. Accessed 1 April 2020.

57 This was his slogan for Reagan's 1984 re-election campaign.

58 Business is here measured as gross domestic investment, which declined by 0.7 percentage <https://fred.stlouisfed.org/graph/?g=kag2>

59 Ronald Reagan quoted in Lou Cannon (2003) *Ronald Reagan: The Presidential Portfolio*. New York: Public Books, p. 128.

It is easy to take a cheap shot at Ronald Reagan for this. Political opponents have seen all this as evidence that 'Reaganomics failed'[60]. That would be unfair. Reagan was unable to deliver on his promises because he was in a constant battle with Congress. The problem was not Ronald Reagan but the system. Presidentialism was the cause of his failure to deliver.

The balance sheet for presidentialism is a grim one; inflexibility, lack of clear accountability and gridlock with resulting paralysis are the hallmarks of a system that promises efficiency and offers the opposite.

So what have we learned? Many people were duped into believing that under Mussolini, at least, the trains were on time. They were not. Otherwise sympathetic tour operators were willing to 'make an affidavit to the effect that most Italian trains … were not on schedule – or near it'[61]. But *Il Duce*, a former journalist, knew the power of creating a myth. It was spin. Just like the similar claims by his colleagues ninety years later. The facts, alongside our statistics prove that dictatorship does *not* work.

Despite the many claims that dictatorships 'get things done' the statistical evidence proves otherwise. Neither one-party states nor traditional monarchies, like the ones in the Gulf States, score highly on the Better Place Index. When measured against practically all the other factors, authoritarian states have a poor record. Countries with democratic systems of government are richer.

'Is it not impossible for a people to be well governed, that they are to obey more masters than one?' asked Thomas Hobbes, the English philosopher and enthusiast for the rule by a single man[62]. Hobbes considered the question to be a rhetorical one. It was not. Much as Hobbes was enthusiastic about mathematics, he did not have access to Big Data and statistics as a discipline was yet to be invented. In any case, the answer to Hobbes' question is quite simple, 'no', it is *not* impossible to be governed by more masters. States that are governed by a single individual fare poorly. The data unequivocally point in that direction. And the reasons for this, among

60 Paul Krugman, 'Debunking the Reagan Myth', *New York Times*, 21 January 2008.

61 Bergens Evans (1954) *The Spoor of Spooks: And Other Nonsense*. New York: Knopf, 77.

62 Thomas Hobbes (1969) *Behemoth: Or the Long Parliament*. London: Frans Cass & Co, p. 156.

many things, are that dictators waste money on placating their would-be challengers and that they silence public opinion, and thereby deprive themselves of good and sensible advice. To advocate, say, the Chinese model is not supported by the facts.

Yet, it remains to be seen how – or if – democracies could improve things. For although presidential systems (such as that of the United States) did not do quite as badly as dictatorships, that too was found wanting. So, can democracies improve public policies? Are they likely to provide more success?

Parliaments, People and a Better Place

So, what is the alternative? It is clear that authoritarianism doesn't work. But presidential systems, for all the reasons we have shown, simply don't work, either. So, could it be that political institutions are just not that important that it all down to having the economic policies outlined in Chapter 2 (high taxes and a large state), and open borders and cultural homogeneity as we found in Chapter 3?

Some might consider that the failure of presidential government suggests that democracy is as unsuccessful as authoritarian countries. Could that be so?

One problem with this line of argument: It is that there are many other types of democracy than the American model of a president and a Congress. In fact, in Europe only one country – it is tiny Cyprus (with a population just over one million).

But what can we put in its stead? Maybe the debates in an assembly, in a parliament or a legislature are the key to success? Statistics is not everything, but the data suggests that countries with parliaments and prime ministers are better than the ones governed by a president. The Figure 4.4 shows the average BPI for states without a parliamentary system. Countries which are governed by a government that relies on support from parliaments have an average BPI-score of thirty. Those governed by other systems have a BPI of, on average, -14.

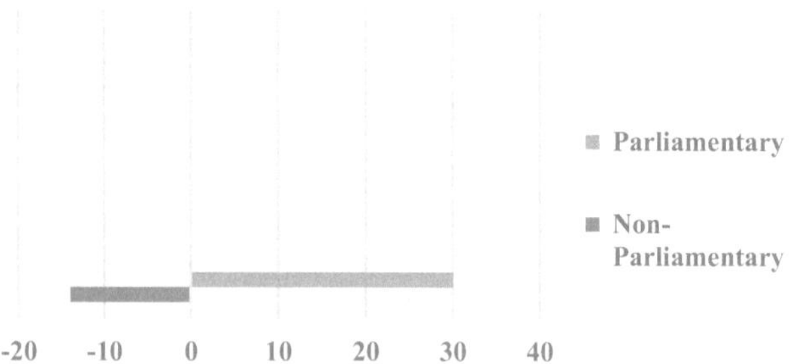

Figure 4.4 BPI in Parliamentary and Non-Parliamentary Systems

This is not coincidental, and the tendency is supported by other types of statistical measures. There is a strong statistical correlation between parliaments and a high BPI-score of 0.44. And the same relationship exists between the GDP and parliamentarism, here with a correlation of 0.43.

Why is it that parliamentary systems are so much better at delivering good policy In the nineteenth century, the future American President Woodrow Wilson (then an academic) cast a wistful eye to the British parliamentary system because it was more efficient; because the House of Commons could act swiftly, and yet be responsible to the electorate. In America – and more generally under a presidential system – there would be gridlock and all the other ills described above. Conversely, under the British system, as Wilson perceived it from across the sea, policies were 'definitely forecast in party programmes and sanctioned by the public voice' in elections. The Parliamentary system, Wilson observed, proved the voters with the 'means for holding them [the politicians] to a faithful execution of those plans in clear-cut Acts of Congress'[63].

But, wait a minute? Isn't that contrary to all the ideas of the American republic? Of checks and balances and the other things the Founding Fathers espoused and defended? Woodrow Wilson, who had a penchant for provocation, would probably not have minded that. It all gave effect to his writings.

63 Wilson, Woodrow (1886) 'Responsible Government under the Constitution'. *Atlantic Monthly*, 57, 542–553, at p. 553.

But for others, this might be of greater concern. What about federalism? About the senate? All these are important points that need to be answered and addressed, especially as they have become almost sacred tracts for many living in the west and even beyond.

When the American Constitution had been drafted in Philadelphia in 1787, a group of young men – most importantly James Madison (a bookish plantation owner from Virginia) and Alexander Hamilton (now the main character in an eponymous Broadway musical) – wrote a series of articles aimed at convincing the voters in New York that they should vote for candidates who would ratify the new constitution. The result of the articles – which were published later – became known as The Federalist Papers and were all signed by the pen name Publius – named after one of one of four Roman aristocrats who overthrew the last king and established a Republic in 509 BC.

The American republic, the world's oldest proper democracy, was based on a number of ideas that deserve to be mentioned. Above all, Publius believed 'internal controls on government would be necessary'[64], lest politicians should get carried away and enact their pet legislative projects – or worse still be encouraged to pass legislation sponsored by lobbyists and well-heeled interests. The word democracy, interestingly, was rarely used. Publius was not too trustful of the people, but nor did he have a lot of faith in the ruling elite. The authors of the Federalist feared – with good reason, we might add – that presidents would usurp powers, that 'men who have overturned republics … have begun their career by paying an obsequious court to the people, commencing as demagogues and ending as tyrants'[65]. Perhaps a rather prescient insight.

The answer to this was to decentralise power, but also to have a senate, a body that in James Madison's words would check the 'propensity of all

64 Madison, James (1961) 'Federalist Paper No. 51', in Alexander Hamilton, James Madison and John Jay (Editors) *The Federalist Papers*. Signet Classics, pp. 317–322, at p. 139.

65 Alexander Hamilton (1961) 'Federalist Paper No. 1', in Alexander Hamilton, James Madison and John Jay (Editors) *The Federalist Papers*. Signet Classics, pp. 27–31, at p. 29.

single or numerous assemblies to yield to the impulse of sudden and violent passions'[66].

The idea was widely shared. The writers who defended the idea of having a Second Chamber, reads like a hall of fame of famous political theorists. In the Victorian age many defended having an Upper House, as the Lower House 'easily becomes despotic and overweening', as John Stuart Mill wrote. And in the beginning of the twentieth century, it was taken for granted in Britain that 'the chief advantage of dividing a legislature into two branches was that the one may check the haste and correct the mistakes of the other'[67].

The break on the haste of the lower chamber – meant that all legislation – would (in theory) be well-considered, and that, as a result, there would be greater prosperity and peace. It's a popular theory. And it has had practical effect. Around the world, seventy countries out of 193 have senates, of which seventeen are in Europe. While all Federal stats have Second Chambers, they are also common in larger states. But do they work?

Woodrow Wilson was certainly challenging rather powerful men, a dominant practice, and the prevailing public opinion when he wrote. So, was he right? Unlike Wilson, we are in the privileged position that we can put the proposition to the test. So, do senates yield better results?

The answer is that countries with senates, second chambers or whatever we call them, are marginally worse off in terms of the BPI, though the relationship is not statistically significant[68]. Likewise, there is absolutely no correlation between GDP per Capita and having a senate[69]. So, senates just don't add anything to the mix, and they certainly do not improve the quality of legislation. Jean-Jacques Rousseay, another prominent observer

66 Madison, 'Federalist Paper No. 62', in Alexander Hamilton, James Madison and John Jay (Editors) *The Federalist Papers*. Signet Classics, pp. 374–380, at p. 377.

67 John Stuart Mill and James Bryce quoted in Samuel C. Patterson and Anthony Mughan (1999) 'Senates and the Theory of Bicameralism', in Samuel C. Patterson and Anthony Mughan (Editors) *Senates: Bicameralism in the Contemporary World*. Columbus: Ohio State University Press, pp. 1–31, at p. 13.

68 R= -0.061 Margin of error plus/minus 0.165, based on 518 cases.

69 R =0. 005 with a margin of error of 95 percent. Based on 508 cases.

on this matter, observed 'qu'a force de délibérer on perd souvent le fruit de la deliberation – 'by dint of deliberation we often lose the fruits thereof'[70].

Possibly so, we don't know the finer points, but the fact remains that there is naught statistical argument for believing that second chambers improve legislation. Many countries with second chambers, to be sure, are successful, among them Switzerland, to name but one; however a larger number are not, for example, Norway, Luxembourg, Denmark.

There have been no fewer arguments for decentralisation of powers – the type of power-sharing that is known as federalism, which we know from America, Canada, Australia and the Federal Republic of Germany. At its core, this 'is a political organisation in which the activities of government are divided between regional governments and a central government in such a way that each kind of government has some activities on which it makes final decisions'[71]. It is also one where the 'allocation of powers derives from the constitution and cannot be unilaterally changed by either set of legislators'[72].

The argument, once again, is that it prevents the tendency of 'power to corrupt and absolute power to corrupt absolutely'[73]. A federation, technically speaking, is a system where the different levels of government (the central as well as the regional) have powers prescribed and protected by the constitution, and that they, through this, 'enjoy the goodness of the internal government of each one, and with regard to the exterior ... has the force of association, the advantages of larger monarchies'[74]. That is the theory, at least. In practice there is only a moderate correlation between

70 Jean-Jacques Rousseau (1964) 'Du Contrat Social', in Jean-Jacques Rousseau: *Œuvres completes III, Écrit Politiques*. Paris: Gallimard, pp. 347–470, p. 402.

71 Riker, W. H. (1975) 'Federalism', in F. Greenstein & N. Polsby (Editors) *Handbook of Political Science: Governmental Institutions and Processes*. Reading, MA: Addison-Wesley Publishing, p. 101.

72 Marshall, G. (1991). 'Federalism', in David Miller et al. (Editors) *The Blackwell Encyclopaedia of Political Thought*. Oxford: Blackwell, at p. 151.

73 Lord Acton, Letter to Archbishop Mandell Creighton, 5 April 1887.

74 Charles Montesquieu (1951) [1748] 'De L'esprit des Lois', in *Montesquieu: Œuvres* Complétes. Paris: Gallimard, p. 371.

GDP per Capita and federation, and there is simply no correlation between the Better Place Index and this type of territorial governance[75].

So then Woodrow Wilson was correct, though his proposition was, when you look closely, that the British Parliament is effective, because it is likely to get things done, and because it has, at the same time, a democratic mandate.

There is a lot to be said for the British system, also known as the Westminster System or the Majoritarian Model[76]. Woodrow Wilson did not go into detail about this system, and admittedly, his article was written a long time ago. Back then there were not a variety of parliamentary systems we have at the beginning of the twenty-first century.

Those looking at institutions today, point out a number of other features of the Westminster System. One of them is that governments almost always have a majority, and that this chiefly is a result of the so-called *First-Past-the-Post electoral system*, in which you only get represented in the legislature if you are able to win most votes in a constituency (or a precinct, to use the American word for it). In Britain, and in other countries like Canada, Australia, Jamaica and Barbados, this system tends to ensure that one party has a majority of the members in the legislature.

Critics will note that this system does not guarantee that a majority in parliament represents the majority of the votes. For example, a powerful prime minister like the Conservative Margaret Thatcher in Britain never won more than 43 percent of the votes, and on the other side of politics, the Canadian Liberal firebrand Pierre Trudeau never achieved more than 45 percent of the popular vote. Thus, in many ways, the Westminster System is a system of government by the largest minority. This might be unfair, undemocratic even, and one prominent critic felt that this system went against the ideal that 'it is an essential part of democracy that minorities should be adequately represented'[77].

75 GDP per Capita and Federation. R= 0.18 (with a margin of error of 0.01 percent, based on 518 observations). BPI and Federation, Correlations R=0.047, with a margin of error of plus/minus 28 percent (both based on 518 observations).

76 Arend Lijphart (2012) *Patterns of Democracy. Government Forms and Performance in Thirty-Six Countries*. New Haven: Yale University Press.

77 John Stuart Mill (1991) 'Considerations on Representative Government', in John Gray (Editor) *On Liberty and Other Essays*. Oxford: Oxford University Press, pp. 203–467, at p. 307.

Those who are opposed to the Majoritarian System with its First-Past-the-Post elections will suggest one of several alternatives, collectively known as Proportional Representation. The finer points are complicated even to political scientists, but the basic gist is that parties get represented in proportion to the number of votes they receive. In this way, John Stuart Mill, wrote in a famous analysis, the 'minority groups would have precisely the amount of power which they ought to have'[78]. The result of this is that no party is in overall control, and that the parties must form coalitions and negotiate and find compromises that everyone can live with, and which protect the most significant groups in society from the tyranny of the majority.

In some countries, such as Ireland, people are allowed to have several votes, which are then divided up[79], but in most countries that have proportional representation, the voters only have a single vote, which they can cast for a party or candidate. The party then gets a share of the vote that is proportional to the size of the voting area. Again, all this can be rather complicated, and the system is not entirely 'proportional'. In some countries, for example, the Netherlands and Israel, where the whole country is one large single constituency, the system is perfectly proportional. In other countries, such as Denmark, Switzerland and Austria, the countries are divided into a number of constituencies from which several representatives are chosen. The more members are chosen from each of these constituencies the more proportional the system. While not perfect these countries come much closer to representing minorities than under the Majoritarian System, and it is virtually impossible under these systems to have government by the largest minorities.

To make matters even more complicated, some countries have a bit of both worlds. For example, in Germany and Italy, voters vote for both individual candidates (as in the Westminster system), and have a second vote for a political party. In this way, the system can be broadly proportional – or fair – and at the same time the votes can choose a local representative.

78 John Stuart Mill (1991) 'Considerations on Representative Government', p. 323.

79 This so-called 'preferential system' is known as The Single Transferable Vote. On electoral systems generally see: Soudriette, Richard W., and Andrew Ellis (2006) 'Electoral Systems Today: A Global Snapshot'. *Journal of Democracy*, 17(2), 78–88.

But if the focus is on creating efficient government – if we focus solely on policy outcomes – does such a proportional system work? Basically, does it lead to a higher BPI-score? Some think not. They have even suggested that the Majoritarian System is better at producing efficient governments that get things done, bluntly because the supposedly endless negotiations and haggling over compromises can be done away with[80].

Once again, the proof lies in facts and not in hearsay; in statistics and not in second-guessing. So, we need a statistical measure, not because politics can be an exact science, but because numbers provide us with a good starting point for a more detailed analysis. How can we do this? Without going into the finer points, one can divide the different systems into three categories the pure proportional systems (Switzerland and Ireland), the Mixed-Members Systems (Germany and New Zealand) and the Majoritarian Systems (in different forms those of France, Australia and the United Kingdom). And to quantify this, we can give two points to the first category, one to the second and naught to the last. We can then use this crude index to measure which countries do best on the Better Place Index.

So, what do we get? Is the Westminster System more efficient? In fact, it is not. The opposite if anything, is true. Unlike the conventional wisdom that this system brings more stable government and more efficiency, it is the other way round. The more proportional systems are slightly more likely to produce economic growth, and they are massively more likely to have a higher BPI[81].

Why do we see such correlations? In some ways, it is nothing new. Research from earlier epochs has suggested a similar tendency, though only based on a narrow sample of established democracies. Perhaps the reason is that successful government 'requires not so much a strong hand as a steady one and that proportional representation and coalition governments are better able to provide centrist policy making'. For, as we saw in

80 T. Persson and G. Tabellini (2003) *Economic Effects of Constitutions*. Cambridge, MA: MIT Press.

81 The correlations are, respectively, proportional electoral systems Iand BPI: R=0. 32, With a margin of error of less than 0.001 percent based on 494 cases. The correlation between PR and GDP per Capita is positive but only R= 0.19 with the same margin of error and based on the same number of cases.

Chapter 2, this moderate form of economic policy making is conducive to better outcomes on all fronts. And, hence it is that 'policies supported by a broad consensus are also more likely to be carried out and to remain on course than policies imposed by a "decisive" government against the wishes of important sectors of society'[82].

This line of reasoning is not only proved by the fact that eight out of ten of the highest scoring countries on the Better Place Index are, what is called *Consensus Democracies* with proportional electoral systems, it is also supported by direct experiences. Erling Olsen, a former economics professor who became Speaker of the Danish Parliament, reflected on his experiences in a small country with many political parties and very proportional electoral system,

> It may surprise many that Denmark, not in spite of but because of its minority governments, has achieved such a level of political stability. Quite simply, most laws survive elections. We change governments more often than we change policies. It is also remarkable that even our rare majority governments reach out and seek broad agreements. They do so out of necessity, as a slim majority might tempt certain members to get media attention by defying the party-line. A government can fire-proof itself against this by seeking broad agreements that make such actions by individual parliamentarians uninteresting[83].

'What men call chatter what's really matter,' the actor Bob Hoskins told the audience in his trademark cockney accent, in a phone commercial in the 1990s[84]. The same is true for political institutions. As he also said, 'It's good to talk'.

82 Lijphart *Patterns of Democracy,* p. 257. Pippa Norris found the same but was not able to find correlations overall between democracy and growth. Based on the data after 2010, a different picture emerges. Democracy is now strongly correlated with economic growth and with the BPI. P. Norris (2012) *Making Democratic Governance Work: How Regimes Shape Prosperity, Welfare, and Peace*. Cambridge University Press.

83 Erling Olsen, quoted in M. Qvortrup (2012) 'Introduction: The Authoritative Allocation of Values: Policy Outcomes and Political Institutions'. *European Political Science*, 12(2), 224–228, at p. 226.

84 <https://www.youtube.com/watch?v=vnHQp2ukDD4>

Famous Last Words

When I first presented these findings at an on-line conference for the Academic Council of the United Nations, the organisers told me it was a bit too abstract.

In my abstract, I had written that I would use multivariate regression analysis and measure the importance of the different factors using b-variables. And, I have to admit, that does sound a bit daunting for the uninitiated.

Basically, b-variables enable you to measure which factors are important. The higher the number, the more important.

So, I made a drawing, which I kept. It looks like this .... And, no, I have not decided to take up abstract art!

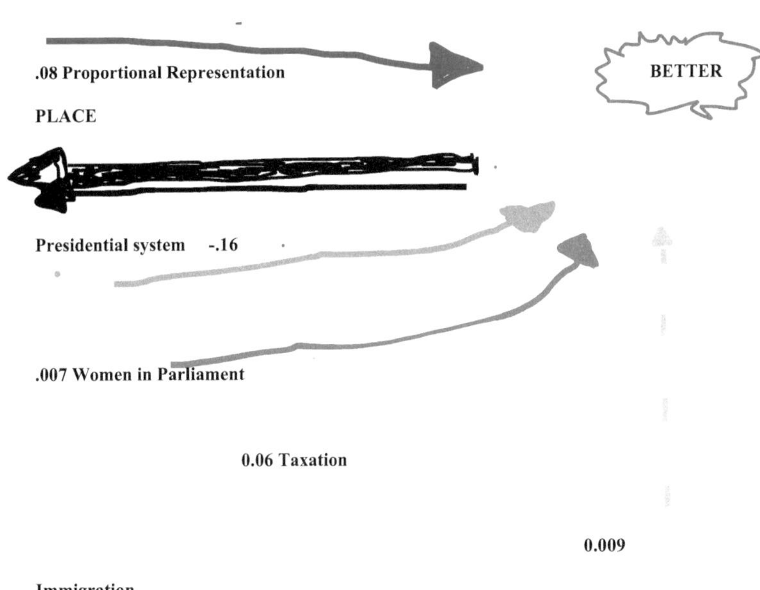

Figure 5.1: Graphic Representation of Factors (B-Variables)

Basically, the arrows show some of the factors that are important for making a 'better place'.

For example, the fat black arrow shows that there is a massive negative relationship between having a presidential system and scoring highly on the BPI.

The other arrows, however, are positive; more women MPs, immigration, high taxation and having an electoral system based on proportional representation are positives. No one at the UN conference objected – perhaps because they rather liked these findings. However, there were grumbles when I mentioned that multi-ethnic societies fare poorly.

That is the nature of writing about policy and politics. People like to be confirmed in their preestablished opinions. Changing your mind is not easy. Nevertheless, if democracy is to prevail, we need to keep an open mind.

Needless to say, this little book is not the final word on the subject of public policy. It is a small attempt to see if statistical evidence (and social science theories) can be used to determine which countries do best, and why.

It was based on openness. On the ideal of *wertungsfrei* – value neutrality – research that was so cherished by the sociologist Max Weber[1].

And, yet there were findings that readers who identify with the political right will welcome. These will gleefully observe that the statistics show that to be successful economically, educationally and environmentally requires that the members of society share the same 'narrative' and are unified around a national identity.

But apart from this finding, the results read like a liberal's paradise, or – if I may put it thus – *The Guardian* reader's wet dream.

For starters, higher taxes are good. Numerically speaking, you add 0.17 years to your life for every extra cent out of a Dollar you pay in taxes. Moreover, there is a statistical tendency that higher taxes reduce the level of CO_2 emissions.

Consistent with this, a large public sector is beneficial for a country's success. In pure numerical terms, for every one percent increase in the public sector's share of GDP children get 0.7 more years of schooling.

1 W. Hennis, U. Brisson and R. Brisson (1994) 'The Meaning of' "wertfreiheit" on the Background and Motives of Max Weber's "postulate"'. *Sociological Theory*, 12(2), 113–125.

A large public sector also makes you live longer; a one percent increase in the size of the public sector adds 0.2 years to your life.

When we use so-called *manifesto scores*, we find that countries that are ideologically to the left do better than those with a centre-right bend. All of this, perhaps explains, why literally everything gets better if countries are more equal. Thus, there are more doctors in more equal societies (a correlation of 0.44). Likewise, there is also a positive correlation between the number of hospital beds per 1,000 people and equality. And more equality also translates into fewer murders.

The aforementioned Max Weber argued, that countries were more likely to be prosperous if the majority of the population were Protestants. The famous relationship between the legendary 'protestant ethics' and 'the spirit of capitalism', was, as we pointed out, not a simple one. But, might there still be a connection between religion and policy outcomes?

Sadly yes, but not in a good way. Sure, Jesus told a rich man, 'Go and sell that thou hast, and give to the poor, and thou shalt have a treasure in heaven' (Matthew 12:21), and the Pope and other Christian leaders rail against inequality. But the majority Christian countries are not good at looking after the poor, or at least of creating equality. Statistically, the fact remains that there is a correlation between inequality and the proportion of Christians of 24 percent.

Though on a more positive note, there is a negative correlation between homicide and the percentage of Christians in a society. So, at least majority Christian countries follow the commandment, 'Thou shalt not kill' (Exodus 20:13) – though that, of course, is as much a Jewish commandment as a Christian one!

Yet, it is not just the Christians who are unsuccessful. The correlation between the percentage of Hindus in a society and GDP per Capita is a negative -33. Moreover, there is a small negative correlation between the proportion of Hindus and the score on the Better Place Index (-0.22). Likewise, the relationship between the percentage of Muslims in a country and the score on the Better Place Index is also negative. But not by much. The correlation between BPI and the proportion of adherents to Islam is -0.28.

Conversely, nonbelievers will be pleased to read that the GDP per Capita slightly rises the more religiously unaffiliated citizens there are.

The correlation between economic output and the proportion of agnostics (here measured by those unaffiliated with any particular religion) is positive – at just over 0.34.

Another factor that is often debated – perhaps even more harshly and uncompromisingly than religion – is immigration. The evidence shows that migration is a positive. Simply put, there is a 58 percent correlation between economic growth and the proportion of migrants per 100,000 inhabitants. Statistically this is extraordinarily high, and the sort of association 3very rare in the social sciences.

In the debate about immigration, and its effects on society as a whole, the positions are often polarised, and they are rarely based on a dispassionate analysis. But if we were to look at the matter without prejudice, we find that more immigration is significantly correlated with longer life expectancy (37 percent), with more education (the correlation is 32 percent), and with more hospital beds (25 percent).

Further, the more people that come to a country the more equal it becomes. In raw figures, the correlation is a negative -40, which is very respectable. Immigration means that everybody is better off. For every migrant that enters a country each individual will gain an additional 0.79 US Dollars. That is, for every-one hundred migrants per 100,000 inhabitants, the average citizens gain just under $800.

In recent years, there has been a lot of talk about a democratic recession or democratic backsliding. 'Strongmen' have claimed that they are successful, and some people have fallen for their arguments. Based on the evidence in this book, the authoritarian leaders are simply wrong. They consistently underperform.

Democracy is good for governance. Democratic countries are more successful than non-democratic ones. The less democratic countries are, the poorer the citizens. A one-point drop on the Freedom House Index is associated with a net loss of $297 per citizen. There is a 44 percent negative correlation between dictatorship and economic output. The reason is simple, autocrats are unlikely to get good advice because they tend not to like to hear the truth. Further, they have to bribe people to stay in power.

But what kind of democracy is best? A presidential system? Hardly, there is a negative correlation of -0.47 between presidentialism and the

Better Place Index. Generally, presidentialism is associated with an array of ills. The average income is lower the more presidential the system is. What is more, life expectancy is shorter under more presidential systems, and education is worse.

So, what kind of democracy works? Parliamentarism, it seems. Countries with parliamentary systems do well. There is a strong statistical association between parliaments and a high score on the BPI-Index of 0.44, and we find an almost identical relationship between the GDP and parliamentarism (0.43).

Politics is not an exact science, and perhaps it never will be. But the statistical evidence in this small book is clear. The lesson is that socially equal democracies that allow immigration – integrate the migrants – and which are not overly religious simply do best.

The reader should keep this in mind when she or he goes to vote.

APPENDIX A

The Better Place Index 2018

1. Switzerland	1.4
2. Luxembourg	1.3
3. Norway	1.24
4. Ireland	1.19
5. Sweden	1.09
6. Iceland	1.08
7. Denmark	1.07
8. Singapore	1.07
9. Austria	0.95
10. Germany	0.94
11. Finland	0.91
12. U.K	0.91
13. Israel	0.9
14. Netherlands	0.89
15. Japan	0.88
16. France	0.88
17. New Zealand	0.88
18. Belgium	0.83
19. Malta	0.79
20. Australia	0.77
21. Italy	0.76
22. Cyprus	0.76
23. Slovenia	0.73
24. Canada	0.71
25. Spain	0.71
26. United States	0.71
27. South Korea	0.63

28. Latvia	0.61
29. Lithuania	0.6
30. Portugal	0.6
31. Czechia	0.59
32. Slovakia	0.59
33. Greece	0.57
34. Croatia	0.57
35. Cuba	0.56
36. Hungary	0.55
37. Montenegro	0.52
38. Chile	0.5
39. Poland	0.5
40. Sri Lanka	0.49
41. Romania	0.47
42. Albania	0.46
43. Georgia	0.46
44. Estonia	0.44
45. Armenia	0.43
46. Serbia	0.41
47. Bulgaria	0.41
48. Barbados	0.39
49. Argentina	0.38
50. Belarus	0.38
51. Panama	0.37
52. Lebanon	0.35
53. Costa Rica	0.35
54. North Macedonia	0.34
55. Uruguay	0.34
56. Jordan	0.34
57. Moldova	0.32
58. Samoa	0.32
59. Bosnia	0.32
60. Maldives	0.32
61. Malaysia	0.31
62. UAE	0.31

63. Bahamas	0.29
64. Peru	0.28
65. Tonga	0.28
66. Antigua	0.28
67. Mauritius	0.28
68. Ecuador	0.27
69. Uzbekistan	0.25
70. Kyrgyzstan	0.23
71. Thailand	0.23
72. Azerbaijan	0.22
73. China	0.22
74. Ukraine	0.2
75. Vietnam	0.2
76. Turkey	0.19
77. Oman	0.18
78. Tunisia	0.17
79. Tajikistan	0.16
80. Algeria	0.16
81. Fiji	0.16
82. Seychelles	0.14
83. Paraguay	0.14
84. Grenada	0.13
85. Russia	0.13
86. Brunei	0.12
87. Suriname	0.12
88. Indonesia	0.09
89. Bahrain	0.09
90. Nicaragua	0.06
91. Bolivia	0.06
92. Morocco	0.06
93. Qatar	0.06
94. Philippines	0.05
95. Egypt	0.03
96. Solomon Islands	0.01
97. Vanuatu	0.01

98. St Lucia	0
99. Bangladesh	0
100. Kazakhstan	-0.01
101. Dominican Rep	-0.02
102. Mongolia	-0.03
103. Colombia	-0.05
104. Cape Verde	-0.06
105. SaoTome & P	-0.07
106. Saudi Arabia	-0.09
107. Kuwait	-0.09
108. Mexico	-0.1
109. Botswana	-0.13
110. Nepal	-0.13
111. Cambodia	-0.13
112. Brazil	-0.14
113. Belize	-0.14
114. India	-0.14
115. Guyana	-0.15
116. Gabon	-0.16
117. Libya	-0.18
118. Bhutan	-0.2
119. Guatemala	-0.2
120. Kenya	-0.2
121. Ghana	-0.2
122. Rwanda	-0.21
123. Kiribati	-0.21
124. St Vincent	-0.26
125. Zimbabwe	-0.26
126. Jamaica	-0.28
127. Myanmar	-0.29
128. Timor-Leste	-0.31
129. Madagascar	-0.31
130. Tanzania	-0.32
131. Malawi	-0.34
132. Iraq	-0.35

133. Congo	-0.35
134. Turkmenistan	-0.36
135. Honduras	-0.36
136. Zambia	-0.36
137. Laos	-0.38
138. Namibia	-0.39
139. Uganda	-0.39
140. Senegal	-0.41
141. Cameroon	-0.46
142. Pakistan	-0.46
143. Eswatini	-0.48
144. Djibouti	-0.49
145. PNG	-0.5
146. Liberia	-0.5
147. Ethiopia	-0.5
148. Sudan	-0.5
149. Haiti	-0.52
150. Comoros	-0.52
151. El Salvador	-0.53
152. Angola	-0.55
153. Gambia	-0.56
154. Mauritania	-0.57
155. Togo	-0.59
156. Burundi	-0.61
157. South Africa	-0.63
158. Mozambique	-0.63
159. Eq Guinea	-0.65
160. Guinea-Bissau	-0.67
161. Burkina Faso	-0.67
162. Benin	-0.68
163. Niger	-0.68
164. DR Congo	-0.74
165. Cote d'Ivoire	-0.76
166. Guinea	-0.82
167. Trinidad	-0.86

168. Nigeria	-0.89
169. Sierra Leone	-0.92
170. Mali	-0.99
171. Chad	-1.06
172. Yemen	-1.21
173. Lesotho	-1.26
174. Afghanistan	-1.35
175. C A R	-1.42

PETER LANG
PROMPT

Peter Lang Prompts offer our authors the opportunity to publish original research in small volumes that are shorter and more affordable than traditional academic monographs. With a faster production time, this concise model gives scholars the chance to publish time-sensitive research, open a forum for debate, and make an impact more quickly. Like all Peter Lang publications, Prompts are thoroughly peer reviewed and can even be included in series.

For further information, please contact:

Peter Lang Ltd,
International Academic Publishers,
52 St Giles, Oxford,
OX1 3LU, United Kingdom

To order, please contact our Customer Service Department:

orders@peterlang.com

Visit our website: www.peterlang.com

Prompts include:

Claudia Aburto Guzmán, *Poesía reciente de voces en diálogo con la ascendencia hispanohablante en los Estados Unidos: Antología breve*. ISBN 978-1-4331-5207-8. 2020

Tywan Ajani, *Barriers to Rebuilding the African American Community: Understanding the Issues Facing Today's African Americans from a Social Work Perspective*. ISBN 978-1-4331-7681-4. 2020

Marcilio de Freitas and Marilene Corrêa da Silva Freitas, *The Future of Amazonia in Brazil: A Worldwide Tragedy*. ISBN 978-1-4331-7793-4. 2020

Janet Farrell Leontiou, *The Doctor Still Knows Best: How Medical Culture Is Still Marked by Paternalism*. Health Communication, vol. 15. ISBN 978-1-4331-7322-6. 2020

Clare Gorman (ed.), *Miss-representation: Women, Literature, Sex and Culture*. ISBN 978-1-78874-586-4. 2020

Eva Marín Hlynsdóttir. *Gender in Organizations: The Icelandic Female Council Manager*. ISBN 978-1-4331-7729-3. 2020

Micol Kates, *Towards a Vegan-Based Ethic: Dismantling Neo-Colonial Hierarchy Through an Ethic of Lovingkindness*. ISBN 978-1-4331-7797-2. 2020

Josiane Ranguin, *Mediating the Windrush Children: Caryl Phillips and Horace Ové*. ISBN 978-1-4331-7424-7. 2020

Dylan Scudder, *Coffee and Conflict in Colombia: Part of the Pentalemma Series on Managing Global Dilemmas*. ISBN 978-1-4331-7568-8. 2020

Dylan Scudder, *Conflict Minerals in the Democratic Republic of Congo: Part of the Pentalemma Series on Managing Global Dilemmas*. ISBN 978-1-4331-7561-9. 2020

Dylan Scudder, *Mining Conflict in the Philippines: Part of the Pentalemma Series on Managing Global Dilemmas*. ISBN 978-1-4331-7632-6. 2020

Dylan Scudder, *Multi-Hazard Disaster in Japan: Part of the Pentalemma Series on Managing Global Dilemmas*. ISBN 978-1-4331-7530-5. 2020

Shai Tubali, *Cosmos and Camus: Science Fiction Film and the Absurd*. ISBN 978-1-78997-664-9. 2020

Angela Williams, *Hip Hop Harem: Women, Rap and Representation in the Middle East*. ISBN 978-1-4331-7295-3. 2020

Ivan Zhavoronkov (trans.), *The Socio-Cultural and Philosophical Origins of Science* by Anatoly Nazirov. ISBN 978-1-4331-7228-1. 2020

Peter Raina, *Heinrich von Kleist Poems*. ISBN 978-1-80079-043-8. 2020

Geanneti Tavares Salomon, *Fashion and Irony in* Dom Casmurro. ISBN 978-1-78997-972-5. 2021

Peter Raina, *Doris Lessing: A Life Behind the Scenes*. ISBN 978-1-80079-183-1. 2021

Matt Qvortrup, *Winners and Losers: Which Countries Are Successful and Why?* ISBN 978-1-80079-405-4. 2021